Dissertation Practice

Dissertation Practice: A Journal for Learning is an interactive resource that promotes journaling to engender key dissertation practices, through activities and exercises. It is rooted in the view that students can use journaling to promote thought, and that the privacy of journal entries ensures comfort and familiarity. This personal context, along with the book's open prompts, allows students to engage in extended and alternative thinking.

The practices suggested here offer opportunities to imagine, create, explain, rethink, analyze, and argue for a study. The book includes blank space for students to enter short pieces of writing – such as reflections, examples, range of topics, and sample annotations – to generate and review thought, and includes features such as self-assessment questions, working with your chair boxes, revision practices, and examples of students' work. As a journal of thinking, it allows students to record their thoughts as they materialize into words, provides a safe place for practice and trial, and helps them locate in one place key pieces of writing foundational to their dissertation.

This is an essential resource for students in PhD and EdD programs in the social sciences and education who are using qualitative, quantitative, and mixed methods.

Diane Bennett Durkin is an Adjunct Professor at UCLA, USA. She has taught on UCLA's Educational Leadership Program (ELP) since 2000, and has guided up to 600 students through the dissertation process.

T0384978

Dissertation Practice

A Journal for Learning

Diane Bennett Durkin

Routledge
Taylor & Francis Group

LONDON AND NEW YORK

Designed cover image: zf L / Getty Images

First published 2025
by Routledge
4 Park Square, Milton Park, Abingdon, Oxon, OX14 4RN

and by Routledge
605 Third Avenue, New York, NY 10158

Routledge is an imprint of the Taylor & Francis Group, an informa business

© 2025 Diane Bennett Durkin

British Library Cataloguing-in-Publication Data
A catalogue record for this book is available from the British Library

ISBN: 978-1-032-85804-3 (hbk)
ISBN: 978-1-032-85800-5 (pbk)
ISBN: 978-1-003-51990-4 (ebk)

DOI: 10.4324/9781003519904

Typeset in Optima
by codeMantra

I dedicate this book to my ever-supportive husband, Michael, without whom I could not have taken on this project, and to my daughter, Celia, who is the family inspiration.

Contents

Acknowledgments

The foundation of this book is the writing of my students, and I would like to acknowledge how their depth and seriousness have inspired this project. They have shared with me, and with other classmates, their processes and struggles and then allowed me to share pieces of their writing with a larger audience. Most important, they have shown me in just what ways writing is learning – it is anything but just a final product on the page.

I would also like to acknowledge the extraordinary support and professionalism of my Routledge editorial team, in particular Eleanor Taylor and more recently Lucy Kennedy and Maddie Gray. In addition, Matt Bickerton has, through two books now, been of wonderful help – in ways too numerous to list. The production team headed by Sugandhi Gnanaprakasam has been on top of the project from the beginning. Overall, the team has always been so positive that I have had free rein to write this book from my deepest and most enduring convictions.

A great debt is owed to my reviewers, especially to Dr. Jeanne Gunner, who in her positive, quizzical, and supportive way, allowed me to rethink some key content and positionings. I am also indebted to my two other supportive reviewers, who gave me valuable insight into how the book might be used in the classroom.

Finally, once again I want to acknowledge the role of my family in this endeavor. My husband was incredibly supportive and listened to me talk my way through key decisions. My daughter Celia, having just produced her own dissertation, was a constant reminder of how difficult this work is. She has been eternally supportive.

Introduction

Writing a dissertation, while hard, is doable, and this journal practicum helps engage you in activities to support this work. But let's start with what dissertation writing is not, to clear away some mothballs.

Writing a dissertation is not sitting down to write as a last step in a standard study protocol. Such a view would assume preset writing skills, and a group of buttons to press, to merely record what you did and found. In contrast, a dissertation involves writing processes that are complex and interwoven with thinking – from start to end. These processes begin before students even consider their topics.

This practicum makes actionable and more widely applicable the advice from my *Writing Strategies for the Education Dissertation* (2021). It provides context, mindsets, kinds of writing, processes, and concrete practices that will get you writing and move you forward. It not only offers writing applications but also explains how these practices help you think about and understand your topic, even if you are not close to deciding on a topic. The activities strive to change attitudes and approaches to writing, for the dissertation and beyond.

The book serves as a kind of working journal. It creates spaces for you to enter short pieces of prompted writing – such as reflections, examples, range of topics, and sample annotations – to generate and review thought. This trail of thought will capture, for later review, some of the key markers of where you are going and where you have been.

Many students come to their dissertations with concerns about producing this extent of academic writing. In the past, they have found that their confidence rises and falls with different writing assignments. Most students, if not all, have never written a dissertation before: They often have little experience with extended writing. As a result, many get to the dissertation stage and are brought up sharp by the complexity of this task, leaving the academy before completing their degree. This journal practicum confronts such a blockage. It gets you writing early and often, breaks up writing tasks, encourages freewriting, and aims to give you the experience and confidence to keep writing. As a journal of your thinking, it records your thoughts as they materialize into words, provides a safe place for practice and trial, and helps you locate in one place key pieces of writing foundational to your dissertation.

Writing as a convergence of thinking, talking, and reading

When we write, we express our attitudes, our thinking, our talk, our previous knowledge, and the new knowledge that forms as we read and reassess. This chapter helps you use a wide scope of mental actions as you first approach your dissertation writing. The early practices described here start with attitudes – an entry-point earlier than the typical "prewriting" stage, where the writer is sketching out, dictating, outlining, drawing, or otherwise producing written plans. *Positive attitudes encourage you to get set.* They help you establish a growth mindset, reconsider the role of error, engage in reflective reading as a form of writing, and welcome writing as a process. They thus encourage wide-ranging but generative activities, including talking with others and using reflective reading and personal experience to identify and define a topic.

Part 1: Getting set

An overview

Getting ready to write is arguably the most important yet overlooked part of the writing process. For this reason, a significant time below is devoted to readying you as to how you think about writing.

DOI: 10.4324/9781003519904-1

Mindset

Let's start with **mindset**. This is where you start – before even opening your computer, **before you even consider topics**. Your attitude and mindset before writing affect your processes and your experience.

Practices

A self-assessment: Write down your thoughts in response to the following:

1. Quickly write 5–6 words or phrases that come to mind when you first think about **writing a dissertation**.

2. What specific experiences, thoughts, or people surface when you think about academic writing (or any kind of assessed writing)?

3. Do you think of writing as a talent that some people have and others don't? What example(s) comes to mind?

4. What words and images in your answers above suggest that you hold a mostly **fixed mindset** about dissertation writing (that people have a fixed capability)? (To decide, notice words or phrases like *not good at writing, always make errors, not my kind of writing, not my talent.*)

5. What words and images suggest you hold a mostly **growth mindset** (that people have an expanding capacity)? (Note words like *challenging, will learn, looking forward to more training, revising helps, willing to work at it, not always fun but I am improving.*)

---

6. Do you ever sit down to write not knowing what you will say? If so, what has that experience been like? Use adjectives to describe it.

7. Have you ever deliberately set out to use writing to think, say about a complicated experience you want to understand? Explain.

8. Share your answers with several classmates. What do your shared experiences suggest to you? What underlying views of writing do you think help in dissertation writing? What new views and behaviors do you think might help you?

Our mindset influences our behavior. Mindset (Dweck, 2006) turns on whether we believe we can improve or not; whether only certain people have an innate talent, while others do not; whether we can learn how to actually write a dissertation or not (supposedly because other people are just plain smart).

Such globalized thinking can undermine students' work. Research shows that those with a growth mindset spend more time, persist through failure, learn more, and accomplish more than those with a fixed mindset. Research on *writer's block* links it to a fixed mindset, leading to damaging self-assessments when writing does not flow: Students say to themselves, "I am not a good writer." This negative self-appraisal is not a good place from which to start a dissertation.

Unsurprisingly, procrastination, defined as behavior that is *needless, counterproductive, and delaying* (Schraw, Wadkins, & Olafson, 2007), follows on the heels of such a view. Procrastination may be a coping mechanism, to relieve stress when starting or completing a complex task such as writing. And this stress leads to avoidance behaviors (Fiore, 2006). Understanding this cycle may help you. Keep in mind that research on our brain's neuroplasticity, throughout our lifespan, contradicts such notions of fixed capacities. It confirms that we are constantly creating new neuronic connections. In first approaching the idea of a study, you need a growth mindset.

More practices

1. **Name** two examples of writing you did that you like (a letter, a poem, a thank you).

2. **Write:** What did you like about that piece of writing?

3. **Brainstorm:** What thoughts do you have when your writing does not flow? What thoughts might be better in terms of growth mindset?

Getting set by talking to others

A specific piece of writing does not have to start at the computer keyboard – it can start with everyday speech. Writing is not very different from speaking, in its relation to thought. The two are intertwined. We don't think full thoughts and then later find the words to speak or write them. Mostly, we start to talk, and as we speak, new thoughts arise. Speaking can thus help us shape (give voice to) our writing, as we are constantly merging thoughts and words, creating ideas as we go.

Students often find that speaking their ideas to another person helps them clarify their thinking: They are surprised to hear what they end up saying. This surprise suggests that they did not fully know what they thought until they heard themselves saying it. Often, on-the-spot speech clarifies weeks of writing attempts, and students regret the lack of a recording. The spoken words, created for others, came out clean and precise. If you already have a topic of interest, the speaking exercises below may help you clarify it:

Practices

1. **In a short, recorded exchange**, explain to a classmate what you might like to study. Let your explanation expand as you talk, or let it expand in response to your classmate's questions.

2. Use driving time to **record** your thoughts. Non-sequential ideas are fine as they promote further thought. Talk to yourself often.

3. Ask to **record** exchanges you have with faculty, thought partners, Chairs, or anyone else who may engage with you verbally. The language you use in context can prove helpful later.

4. Use opportunities to tell people outside of academia about your potential study, what you want to find out. **Write a reflection**: How did your talk help you clarify what you want to study?

Getting ready by de-emphasizing errors (understanding barriers)

When you sit down to write your thoughts, don't be concerned with errors. Easy to say, perhaps: You have likely noted that while writing and speech align, writing differs in being a highly visible system, with any error amplified. Indeed, dissertation writers sense pitfalls everywhere for error – not only at the word, phrase, and sentence levels (e.g. spelling, punctuation, word choice, subject–verb agreement, run-ons) but also at the level of argument (e.g. transitions, citing evidence, connectedness). To get past these anxieties, first off know that error is a natural part of all language learning and production.

Research in first language acquisition teaches us about the innate role of error: The young child first learns to apply a general rule like add "ed" to create past tense (*I jump-ed*) and then overapplies it (*I go-ed*). This over-application is effective rule-based learning, with exceptions learned last (e.g. *I went*). Applied linguistics research further shows that a second language learner applies rules in the same order, with the same effect: big rules first, exceptions last. For instance, present tense (e.g. *I go*) may for some time extend to both present and past tenses (*I go to the store yesterday*). Generalizing errors is natural to the language learner, whether in speech or in writing. But some errors remain *fossilized*. Still, these errors convey signs of language learning.

In writing, many small but persistent (fossilized) writing errors surface that are easy to predict and later eradicate. Here are a few:

1. **It's,** as with: *He cut it's length by two inches.* (Here, we see the writer overgeneralizing the possessive **its** to appear like other possessives, such as **John's**).
2. Their, they're, and there. For example, *Their on the grass I see your book...* (The possessive "their" is overgeneralized to cover the adverb **there**, given the possessive context of "your" book).

Other errors – word choice, spelling, syntax – similarly arise because the system is complex, and the writer's overgeneralizing is not always transparent. But these minor errors are natural to the process and gradually fade out. Foremost, writers need to write their thoughts and not worry about sentence-level error. They can save that for the editing stage.

Practices revealing the logic of error

A practicum follows – one that will help you see the logic of small but, at times, befuddling errors (so that you can forget errors until the editing stage):

1. Look at an early draft of any piece of writing and identify two errors. **Write** the sentences in your journal.

2. Try to create an explanation of that error. **Write:** What logic or general rule might account for that "error"?

3. **Reflect:** How does thinking about the *logic* of an error help you to recognize it?

4. **Reflect:** What strategies might help you get over worrying about errors?

5. Try a 10-minute **quick-write** journal entry on any topic. Don't stop to correct an error. What did you learn about typical production errors?

6. **Reflect:** What strategies helped you to de-emphasize error when producing writing?

In sum

Getting set, then, is not about preparing yourself and your desk for a combat with syntax. It is about resetting your attitude toward language use generally – as a human being whose brain is prewired to learn and use language. Belief in a growth mindset, readiness to use speech to create thought, and reseeing error as a sign of learning will help get you started.

Part 2: Reflecting, reading, and writing to create a big step forward

Overview

Time spent inventing – thinking, reading, pre-writing – offers varied opportunities to design a study. You can start anywhere, but most researchers start with reflection and reading. They then use targeted reading to generate topics and make decisions.

Initial reading and reflecting

Because a credible dissertation involves years of work, you want to begin with an open mind about your topic. Reflecting, and then reading widely, creates multiple possibilities. Skimming diverse lines of research, and summarizing key pieces, may help you identify a topic. While such openness may create uncertainty, most researchers understand the importance of not narrowing too soon.

So where does one start? One can start with a general research interest, a broad sense of something one wants to get involved in. Or one can start with lifelong, cumulative experiences, for which one seeks a frame and a direction. The two sources can also work together to drive you forward.

Invention practices to identify a topic

1. **List** three topics that drive your interest.

2. **Describe** an experience underpinning each. What do you want to know further?

While uncertainty about a topic may feel like swimming without a shoreline in view, listing possible topics is a step forward. Once written, the topics look different – subject to reflection. But don't stop with the obvious. Name a few more possible topics.

More practices

1. **List** three more potential topics. These might be narrower topics. What do you wonder about each?

2. **Write** a few sentences on the practicality of each – why you think each might be workable and why not. How important is the exact topic to you?

Using writing to reflect, decide, and govern reading

Below are some additional practices to help you generate deeper under-standings – to tie potential topics to experience and to motivation – and thus to probe the source of your commitment. A resulting list, tied to research as well as personal meaning, can steady you through the extended time on this project. This writing is likely meant only for yourself.

Practices

1. Do a quick literature search on any three of the above topics, just reading abstracts. Using what you have read, **speed-write** a para-graph on your feelings and experiences about each topic. Do this as notes to yourself.

2. On rereading what you wrote, **rank the topics** in terms of your interest, knowledge, commitment, and resources. **Write:** Why is this topic a good choice for you?

3. For this chosen topic, perform a deeper search for promising studies. Look for a narrower, researchable problem (a specific problem you can investigate, at sites that are accessible). **Write:** What possibilities did you uncover? If you reach a dead end, try another topic.

4. **Write:** Given a chosen problem that lies within your topic, what related questions seem most on researchers' minds recently?

5. **Create** an overview of some key research on this problem.

6. **Write:** Has your interest in this topic/problem changed? What new thoughts do you have?

In sum

Topics of interest change. This early discovery time allows you the freedom to explore, write, change your topic, imagine different projects, and learn what others are doing. Importantly, try to avoid landing on an investigation too soon.

Part 3: Navigating sources: reading with a purpose

Overview

As noted above, reading underlies and informs writing. But how does one choose what one reads, once one singles out a topic? Research librarians can help you identify sources. But how do you determine if a source is worth your effort? This section is about how you evaluate sources, locate a gap, and begin strategizing your Literature Review.

Evaluating sources

If you are following a line of research that matches your interests, you need to *evaluate* the sources you are gathering. A key distinction is whether you are reading empirical, juried studies or whether you are reading position papers – opinions and reasoning but not actual studies that have detailed methods and data. Juried means that the study was sent out to review by experts in the field. Below are some guidelines for credible sources and a follow-up practicum. The focus here is on empirical work.

Practices (for a quick evaluation of sources)

1. Locate one empirical and one positional article. **Write:** What distinguishes the two?

2. **Take Notes:** What kind of data did the empirical study use? How extensive were the data? Why did you choose this study?

What follows are guidelines for identifying key sources.

Identifying the most credible empirical sources

- The source is published by a credible outlet: a well-respected journal in the field or a key publisher of academic work.
- The source is recent, peer reviewed, and often cited; the authors are verifiable experts.
- The source uses empirical data (using quantitative, qualitative, or mixed methods); the data derive from openly discussed methods and reasons for those methods.
- It specifies the research question(s) or purpose.
- It offers a Literature Review to support the gap the study fills, or why the study needed to be done. The references look credible and substantial.
- The study has a reasonable sample, given its methods. (Too few participants with the same demographics may raise questions.)
- The study ties the empirical data to the findings; it also addresses the possibility of other interpretations.
- It analyzes and interprets the data without bias, an agenda, researcher self-interest, or funding from a political organization or agency.
- The work's Discussion links closely to the data, without editorializing, pontificating, or otherwise inflating those findings.

Looking to defend a problem, based on strong sources

Once you have credible sources, they then help you further narrow to a specific project. Identifying a topic, narrowing to a researchable problem, and continuous reading go hand in hand. To narrow, you need to locate **a gap** in the research, or a unique problem of practice, that your study can target. This narrowing likely means that you consider groups of credible studies together. You ask, how do these studies indicate the need for additional work in the area?

Practices: synthesizing studies to locate a gap

1. Choose three juried, empirical studies on a potential topic. In your journal, **write:** How do these three studies, reviewed together, identify a problem you might further investigate?

2. Skim the references from the three studies. **Reflect:** Taken together, what seem to be the key questions these researchers are asking?

3. **Take notes:** Do the three studies suggest a gap (a next step) that needs to be filled? Do the researchers themselves identify next steps? What are these?

Working with your Chair: writing with a purpose

Proposing a study typically involves sharing a short paragraph with your Chair about what you want to investigate and how key sources support your idea. You want to receive your Chair's approval, as well as to gain an overall direction and additional articles that will further your work. If you don't yet have a Chair, you could use this early research to identify a potential Chair, engage their interest (in a *short* email), and generate an initial meeting.

Practice

Summarize in a practice paragraph a potential study – providing a rationale based on your sources. Then read the project summary aloud to a colleague for their response. Revise if needed, and then submit to your Chair. Assume your Chair will need time to carefully consider your thinking. The response will likely focus your thinking and also push you to create an ongoing annotated bibliography.

Writing an annotated bibliography

Writing an **annotated bibliography** helps you, and those who guide you, to more fully comprehend recent work in the field. You write about individual pieces of research – picking those that identify patterns, confirmations, and a research history. This work solidifies where you enter the conversation: What does each study contribute? What does each leave undone?

To begin, find the most recent juried studies targeted to your project. Then for each write a summary (theoretical frame, research questions, supportive literature, methods, findings, conclusions) and an evaluation (strengths and weaknesses in the above). Your research librarian can help, if you are not finding adequate resources.

The **annotated bibliography** will likely shape your Problem Statement (discussed next), underpin your Literature Review and reference list, and influence your Findings and Discussion chapters. At this stage, it helps you target a possible study.

Practices for grouping annotations to develop your study

1. Use your journal to **create annotations** to five key studies. The annotations may vary in length depending on the article.

2. **Consider in notes:** Are there similar findings from several key studies? How might this convergence help you propose a study?

3. **Reflect and write:** Are there studies that disconfirm or complicate a summary of findings? If so, how do you make sense of the disjunction?

4. **Write:** What gaps do you see from these studies? How might you use these gaps to justify your study?

5. **Sum up** what you have most learned from these five studies. How has your search changed?

Chapter summary

So far, you have gotten set – addressed mindset, used talk to think, reduced anxiety over error, and assessed your personal motivation and interest. Then, you entertained various topics, initiated reading and writing on these topics, learned to evaluate sources, and narrowed to a potential study area. Next, as part of initial writing, you wrote a problem summary for your Chair, started up an annotated bibliography, and used these annotations to direct your further research.

These are all important initial activities that often get ignored. Along the way, you have learned a great deal about the processes involved in writing a dissertation. These initial practices are the groundwork for writing a Problem Statement for your study, the focus of the next chapter.

Practices for the Problem Statement

The Problem Statement introduces and summarizes your study as a whole. Its final version will likely be produced last, but your first version scopes out the anticipated study to present to your Chair.

The Problem Statement has a number of key parts: (1) it opens with the larger context of the problem, with key supportive data; (2) it narrows to a researchable problem, with targeted supportive data; (3) it lists the research questions; (4) it summarizes and briefly defends the Methodology – including design, data collection methods, and site and participants; and (5) it states the study's significance.

At the heart of the Problem Statement lie the research questions. These continue to be refined – up through (and sometimes beyond) your preliminary defense. They govern every part of the study, so practicing them is important. You continue to adjust the questions, along with the rest of this summarizing chapter, in relation to the chapter sections; then, once the study's findings have jelled, you likely return to the Problem Statement once again, to make it more accurately state, upfront for readers, the study's purpose and procedures, in answering your research questions.

Part 1: Key sections of the typical Problem Statement

Overview

While different disciplines and projects generate different approaches to the Problem Statement, some elements seem basic. The elements

DOI: 10.4324/9781003519904-2

below typify empirical studies in education and in the social and behavioral sciences. However, the content and order are not written in stone. Always check with your Chair for required elements.

Background to the problem

The Background section is where, with broad strokes, you likely show the history, pervasiveness, and depth of the problem. There is much leeway for this background, but your goal is to convince readers that significant evidence supports your choice of a problem. You might use national, state, or district data; you could recount a history of failed practices; you might show the effects of certain policies or practices on different populations. One suggestion here, however: Allow the reader to take in the significance of this evidence on their own – avoid overgeneralizing, denouncing, or filling this section with imperatives.

Practices that get the Background section off the ground

1. Skim a number of key data sources for your possible problem. **Write:** What large-scale data most jump out at you?

2. **Write** in a paragraph: What key data unveil the extent of the problem?

3. **Jot down:** What information seems missing in this Background?

4. **Outline** a Background to your chosen problem with key arguments. List studies under each. Leave placeholder statements for later support.

5. **Write a few paragraphs:** Produce a tentative statement of the large-scale (national, state, or district) problem you will investigate.

The researchable problem

The researchable problem is the local or narrowed manifestation of the national or large-scale problem; it is researchable in that you can investigate or redress it – given your resources, timeline, site, population, and access. Here is an example: One might identify, say, the national problem of high dropout rates for African-American high school boys. One student researcher narrowed this problem to the lack of targeted, positive interventions for *street-life* (often gang-related) Black boys in an urban school setting. For his project he designed a school-wide intervention and enacted an action-research study involving key faculty members and a recruited selection of *street-life* Black male students. This study was researchable, it mirrored a national problem, it created and tested an innovative solution, and it charted the growth – as incipient researchers of their own culture – of the Black male participants, alongside their teachers. The project resulted in recommendations for future school-wide interventions.

Practices for innovating

1. **List** 2–3 researchable problems that particularize the broad problem you selected.

2. **Brainstorm:** Choose one, and journal a paragraph on what that researchable problem might look like, and the key data that argue for the need to redress it.

3. **Write:** Choose an additional problem, and write a similar paragraph for it.

4. **Reflect and note in your journal:** What makes one problem more researchable than another? What criteria do you have for choosing your problem?

5. **List:** Identify key research that supports your choice of a researchable problem.

6. **Quick-Write:** Create several paragraphs on the problem you wish to investigate and the evidence supporting the need for your study.

7. **Activity:** Share the chosen problem with a colleague or two. What was their response to your proposed problem? What insights did they bring to the study idea? **Take notes.**

The research questions

As noted, your research questions are key but provisional. Typically, students start with questions too broad or indeterminate to govern their particular study. Expect the questions to be refined as you work with your Chair. But you can also start narrowing and refining on your own.

Here is a typical revision. A student was interested in the benefits of Historically Black Colleges and Universities (HBCUs). He quickly narrowed to how counselors at independent schools advised their Black students about HBCUs. But his key question was not answerable, objectively. He asked:

How knowledgeable are college counselors at independent schools about HBCUs?

The question is both too broad and too subjective. Not being "knowledgeable" could mean a lot of things, mostly judgmental. One cannot objectively determine whether a counselor is "knowledgeable" (a global state of being) unless one begins with a measurable standard of what constitutes being "knowledgeable." Further, the question presupposes a problem with counselors' knowledge, when the student does not yet know that this problem exists: He assumes the very thing that he is testing.

The question was rewritten more objectively to ask:

What information, advice and materials do college counselors at independent schools give to Black students about HBCUs?

This question now forms part of a descriptive study of what independent school counselors actually say, provide, and do (all observable behaviors) when they advise Black students about traditional Black colleges. The data will be less prone to subjectivity and judgment. The student eliminated the indeterminate criterion of "knowledgeable" and substituted the more concrete (and positive) criteria of "advice and materials."

A similar example underscores the need for narrowing: The writer's original question was very broad and could have led to sweeping responses:

What do Latina executives say influenced their decision to pursue a leadership position in their institutions?

The revision focuses the data to be collected:

What work-related decisions, actions, or experiences do Latina executives perceive as having contributed to their advancement to senior positions in a major R1 research institution?

The revision narrows the kind of data she will collect. A sub-question might probe the Latina executives' perceived barriers, to complete the story of leadership for this underrepresented group.

Revision practices

1. **Write** in your journal 4–6 potential research questions. Are any of the questions subjective, depreciating, or overly general? Why? If so, **revise them**.

2. **Take notes:** Share your revised questions with colleagues. What was their response? What kind of data might each provoke? **Revise again**.

3. **Reflection:** Which question(s) best generates objective data, without obvious presuppositions?

4. **Consider:** Could some of your questions become sub-questions? If so, **rewrite question(s).**

Methodology

The Problem Statement includes a brief summary of your methods. As your project develops, this initial description will undergo change. But at this stage, the summary of methods identifies and justifies your *design* (qualitative, quantitative, mixed – or possibly an analysis of existing data); the kinds of *data collected* and examined (interviews, focus groups, observations, surveys, documents, or other data sources) with a brief rationale for each; and the projected *sites* and *populations* (with a brief set of criteria). In this early stage, these are projections. Keep in mind that this initial thinking about methods typically moves forward under the guidance of your Chair.

Self-questioning practices

1. **Reflect and note:** What kinds of information are you most interested in collecting? How would that data help improve present knowledge or current actions?

2. **Write to envision subjects/participants:** What sites or population(s) do you have access to? Would they be representative enough? Do they offer a unique slant on the problem? How will you encourage the potential subjects to participate?

3. **Notes on your reasoning for design:** Are you collecting a wide swath of quantitative data on a fixed set of questions, or are you collecting open-ended, in-depth responses from a narrower group or source? What is the rationale for your choice?

4. **Outline:** Identify potential barriers to collecting your data. How would you surmount each?

5. **Write in your journal** an initial statement and rationale for your design and methods that you think is doable. Share it with colleagues for feedback.

Significance

The Problem Statement typically ends with a brief section on the significance of your investigation: How is this problem important? How will this study contribute to what we know? Again, avoid imperatives here: Stick to what existing research tells us and how your work is needed.

Practices to generate thoughts on significance

1. **Brainstorm a list:** You likely have read studies suggesting benefits. Consolidate the benefits of your study by creating a list.

2. Using your list, **draft a paragraph** on benefits. What contribution does the study make? Who could benefit? Could the study affect policy?

3. **Revise your paragraph on significance:** Open with the most important benefits first; link the points with logical connectors; stay objective.

4. **Write separately your first draft of the Problem Statement.**

Working with your Chair

The Problem Statement is your project in miniature, so you will likely hold key conversations with your Chair as you generate this initial draft. Pay special attention to the advice in this early stage, as your Chair can encourage productive research and ward off dead-end lines of thought. One way to absorb, and show respect for, this highly valuable early brainstorming is to ask to *record all conversations*. Students rarely can take in, respond to, and remember all that transpires in these meetings. But often, the Chair and student together articulate the study – its nature, contribution, possible design, line of research. These moments of insight are mutually generated and do not always repeat. Be sure to collect and value them.

In sum

The Problem Statement typically includes the above sections. However, these don't always present exactly as described here, because different disciplines have their own conventions. Nor are they typically written in a linear fashion, section after section. Whatever the format or process, the Problem Statement eventually presents a summary argument for your study – signaling that it is doable and that it contributes. As the study evolves, these sections undergo change.

Part 2: Review your work (rethinking and reseeing)

Overview

In assessing a developing Problem Statement, readers look to see if the project is clear, doable, free of bias, and methodologically sound. You can review your work with these issues in mind. Clarity and consistency are good places to start. You will also need to review how the pieces fit together to see how, as a whole, the Problem Statement works.

Reworking the inconsistent and the unexplained

Natural inconsistencies and disjunctions occur in the process of writing a Problem Statement. Read the work through, checking for inconsistencies, especially between research questions and data collection methods.

Practices for checking and clarifying

1. For the Problem Statement, **refine** your research questions to fit the kind of empirical data you say you will collect.

2. **Write:** How will the data collected from each method answer a particular research question?
    Explain and **add** a few sentences to your description of each of your selected methods.

3. **Take notes:** Are the sites, participants, and larger geographical locations consistent with the purpose of the study? Explain.

4. **Review** your criteria for site(s) and participants, which typically need more detailing. **Add:** What additional criteria might be important for choosing your site(s) and population?

5. Have you explained your access? **Identify** in your journal any potential barriers.

6. **Revise** (or clarify) your recruitment strategy. What problems might arise? How will you address them?

7. If appropriate, **write** a letter asking a leader at a site to create a memorandum of understanding (MOU) or other statement giving you access.

   A note: Many of the above issues will be revisited when you detail your Methodology chapter, discussed later.

Identifying barriers for later attention

You can't anticipate all the barriers to your study before you initiate it. But anticipating some barriers allows you to detail them and to have a backup plan. Early on, try to brainstorm such barriers, make notes on how to overcome them, and save these notes for when you talk with your Chair. The consequences of not planning ahead are far worse than sharing concerns upfront.

Practice in anticipating barriers

1. **Brainstorm:** List all the potential barriers that might arise for your study (e.g. low recruitment, loss of a site, over-representation by one group or person, lack of geographical diversity, your own positionality).

2. **Write:** What backup plan do you have for site/participants and for data collection methods?

Fitting the pieces together

Rereading your Problem Statement, at various junctures, often reveals places where you can connect and tighten the argument. Reading is a stimulus for writing, so put yourself in the place of your reader. If you were a reviewer, about to fund this research, what potential disconnects would you see?

Practices for rereading to connect

1. **Connecting pieces:** The Problem Statement unfolds as a series of arguments. What points in these arguments seem unrelated? What connectors could help relate the points?

2. **Add** more headings throughout to guide the reader through sections.
3. **Read aloud:** Note in your journal places that need tighter connections. **Revise** those places.

In sum

This section reminds you to continue to review and rewrite the Problem Statement. You have to reread in order to move ahead. Your first task was to get words on the page; the next is rewriting. Remember that rewriting is part of thinking – it does not just fix what is set down. By writing provisional pieces and then reviewing them, you prompt thought and solve problems. Without initial writing, the problems remain in your head, and it is difficult to see solutions.

Part 3: Avoiding early missteps (jumping to solutions, revealing bias, overgeneralizing)

Overview

A number of hidden missteps are commonplace in approaching a problem and should be mentioned here. These missteps are not always easy to recognize, but they can trip you up before you start. These include (1) jumping to solutions before researching the problem (because students want to solve problems), (2) revealing bias (students often think they know the cause of the problem), and (3) overgeneralizing (recalling one or two examples as definitive). These are common missteps, prompted by one's natural desire to solve problems.

Jumping to solutions

A typical misstep is to start writing your Problem Statement with a solution in mind, before investigating and understanding the problem. Take, for instance, the student desiring to solve a problem by having college counselors at independent schools present to Black students the benefits of HBCUs. As noted earlier, he may have assumed a problem – counselors' lack of knowledge – but he did not know for sure that this was the case. Rather, he started with a solution, namely that independent school counselors needed to provide the kind of HBCU advising to their Black students that he had in mind.

To avoid an early leap to solutions, the student needed to pull back from solutions and first gather data on the problem. He needed to detail what counselors are actually doing and plan to adjust his solution to what he discovers is the problem. In the end, he discovered that individual counselors had a wide variety of strategies for informing students of HBCU benefits, strategies particularly responsive to school proximity to HBCUs.

Practices to clarify the problem

1. **Write:** What assumptions are you making, if any, that might prompt solutions before you understand the problem?

2. **Write:** How can you adjust your study so that it does not start with solutions? What new research questions might emerge?

Revealing bias

Bias often surfaces in dissertation work and requires careful examination. Research questions, in particular, often reveal hidden biases. A bias can be an assumption that negatively characterizes a group of people or group of actions. Bias can also appear in the positionality of the researcher, whose role already defines their perspective, interests, and leanings.

Practices to uncover potential bias

1. **Reflect and write:** What potential for bias do you see in your study? What generalizations are you making about groups of people or events that not everyone would agree with?

2. **Reflect:** Do your research questions indicate a bias? What do they assume? Explain.

3. **Consider:** Where else might bias appear in your Problem Statement? (e.g. selection criteria? geographical locations? protocol questions?)

4. **Write:** How will you guard against bias? Explain.

_____

Overgeneralizing

Overgeneralizing is a common misstep, making too much of a small amount of data, jumping from particulars to large-scale recommendations, or assuming that all sites with a few common characteristics reflect the same problems everywhere. Review your Problem Statement. Look for places where you might claim too much. Locate leaps that others might question. Ask colleagues to review your writing for such leaps.

Practices to reduce questionable generalizing

1. **Identify** places in your Problem Statement that might be overgeneralized. **List** some words that seem too broad to be researched. What groups or actions might not be represented in the groupings you have made?

In sum

Looking for missteps is a constant necessity. Researchers naturally want to jump to solutions, they often overgeneralize because their evidence is limited, and they typically exhibit some form of bias, simply in their choices of sites and participants, and in their own perspectives and positions. Discovering where these missteps significantly undermine your study is a natural part of the process of revising your work. Also, it is a key opportunity to learn.

Part 4: Being realistic and practical about time and resources

Overview

A review of your Problem Statement may trigger a different kind of reassessment, one involving your program's requirements, your Chair's expectations, and your personal life. First, find out what is required of you for this degree. How does your Chair scope out your work? Then, be realistic about your own personal constraints in time, access, and resources. If you aggrandize the study, you may not complete it in a timely manner. If you shortchange the work, your Chair may then add unanticipated methods, data, or analyses that were not in your schedule. The advice here is to communicate with your Chair early on, be familiar with similar studies from similar programs, and be realistic about your resources and timeline.

Determining how much data to collect

Data collection from only one source (e.g. participants with a disability, Latina college leaders, or incarcerated adults) and then using one method (e.g. interviews) can result in great depth and focus; however, it can also promote a potentially biased perspective. If other confirming (or disconfirming) data sources are available, consider adding these sources. That being said, you need to assess realistically your time and resources. Your Chair is the ultimate authority here, so you need to discuss what constitutes adequate data for your investigation.

Practices to help you reconsider your data sources

1. **List** all of your projected data sources, in order of importance. What source have you left out? Why did you leave that source out?

2. **Notes:** Compose and pilot a few questions – to explore a source of data you rejected – to see if you are missing quality data.

3. **Write** in your journal: What data will each chosen source likely provide?

4. **Review:** Which data sources are most important to the credibility of your study? Why?

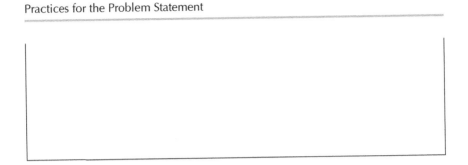

Backward planning

To be realistic about your timeline, it helps to backward map – to plan backward from the date you hope to file your dissertation. But planning from a point that is years in advance may be unrealistic. For a first step, backward plan starting with your Preliminary Orals and the Internal Review Board (IRB) approval, which allows you to get your project underway.

The plan needs to include time for various proposal drafts and revisions; time devoted to scheduling the Orals; two weeks for committee members to read the proposal; time devoted to rewriting parts of the proposal, as required by your Committee at your Orals; and time to submit your proposal to the IRB and to gain its approval.

Practices to assess your timing

1. **Create a backward map**, leading you to a reasonable date for starting your study.

2. **Note:** Reassess your map realistically. Where do you think you may need more time? Why?
3. **Re-plan:** How can you best reduce the loss of time? How can you best use the downtime waiting for responses from your Chair and your committee?

Early contacts: your site(s) and participants

The timeline leading up to your approvals can identify time gaps and specify useful activities. For instance, while your Chair is reviewing a draft, you can review your research or protocol questions. While you await word from IRB, you can expand your Literature Review. Find ways to use any lag time.

During early lag time, try to do some further groundwork to better understand any access, recruitment, or other barriers at potential sites. You might contact potential site leaders to assess their commitment. You could create a MOU where they agree that you can use a site. If developing a survey, you can rework and test out survey questions. These early actions might save you a lot of grief. But each study is different and requires different steps. Some of the practices may apply and others not.

Practices to keep things moving

1. **Create a list** of potential sites and participants.

2. **Create a letter of Introduction:** Write a letter/email to a site administrator explaining your study and asking for access to the site. Have it ready for when you have passed your orals. Be sure a colleague or committee member has reviewed the letter before you send it.

3. **Keep a record** of all contacts.

4. **Write:** After contacting your IRB representative, begin filling out the IRB form. Write some of your responses in your journal, to get going.

5. **Identify** areas that may require special IRB approval. Begin a conversation with those at IRB as to what you will need to certify your study.

Working with your Chair

Your Chair guides you through this pivotal part of your study, paying attention to how you define and support the problem. Discussions need to include research questions and Design, along with data collection methods and potential issues of credibility and bias. Just as important to discuss, though, are practical issues. These include the availability of data, the project scope, timing, as well as your resources. Try to encourage any concrete advice your Chair can give you on these practical issues. It is easy to imagine and propose much more than you can handle. **Write** a list of questions to ask your **Chair**.

Chapter summary

You likely now have produced a draft of the key pieces of your Problem Statement (with early guidance from your Chair), reviewed these pieces for consistency and practicality (as well as for any hidden missteps), and sketched out a plan for getting to and beyond your Preliminary Orals. The practices involved are part of the learning process. Key to moving forward is to keep interweaving writing and reading – to use reading, critical review-ing, and practical actions to shape your project. While your early selection of readings helps define your problem, a broader scope of studies will give the problem context and wide support. The next chapter provides advice and practice on developing and then strengthening the Literature Review.

47

Writing the Literature Review

The Literature Review, like the Problem Statement, is a constantly evolving writing and reading activity. You create provisional arguments, with the literature you already have, and these arguments redirect you toward additional knowledge. *However, many dissertation writers fall down the rabbit hole of delaying writing to extend reading.* The advice here is to let the writing dictate the reading. Without a written document, the thought remains amorphous. The writing practices suggested here embrace the flux of this process but encourage writing to help you move ahead.

Part 1: Arguing for your study: creating, developing, and revising your outline

Overview

As a reminder: the Literature Review is an argument – *it is not a list of related studies.* You do not proceed study by study. Rather, you need to create arguments supporting your project – by first detailing the context of your study, then presenting the existing (perhaps failed) explanations or interventions, and then using those existing studies to argue for why your study is needed. You are making a case. In so doing, you detail, explain, and connect the relevant bodies of existing research to your particular study. You will need an outline and a series of claims. It helps to run that outline past your Chair.

DOI: 10.4324/9781003519904-3

Using what you have

You have already identified and organized some key studies to create your Problem Statement. Reread what you have – to identify what you will expand and what gaps still need to be filled.

Practices: pause so as to build from existing claims

1. Pause for a few minutes and identify three or four claims from your Problem Statement. **Write** each claim in your journal, and place the articles you already cite under each claim. **Add** what claims you still need to make.

---

2. **Identify** more studies and place them under existing or new claims. This might look like a developing outline, with each claim identifying subordinate pieces of evidence and leading to the next claim.

3. **Write several paragraphs in your journal:** Expand the discussion of studies supporting each claim, incorporating new studies.

4. Pause and **add further claims**, if they surface. Reread to assess the development of your argument.

To restate the important point here: The Literature Review is not meant to convince readers that you have read a long list of studies. Rather, it places your study in a research context and argues for its need. To organize your claims, you need to build from an initial outline, integrating the supporting literature.

Developing your initial set of claims into a fuller set

As suggested, it helps to review your Problem Statement argument and then identify your existing claims and evidence. This initial set might then spark thoughts on how to expand. Your more developed set of claims typically operates as a funnel, say from broad national data (e.g. high drop-out rates at community colleges), narrowing to the localized problem and its effects (e.g. underrepresented minority students' lack of belonging). As you state your arguments, and place studies under each claim, you may notice where an argument needs to be broken into sub-arguments – where the research is too thick. The set of claims, when transformed into an outline, will become more multi-tiered. You may also find places where the research is too thin. In this case, you may either continue searching for new evidence or combine sections. This schematizing of the chapter will activate new thought and new searches. It will also help you keep your focus on arguments – not individual studies.

Example of an expanded and logically related set of claims that support a study, opening with the broadest claim

Claim 1: The most basic right of a person with disabilities is the entitlement to a free and appropriate education (IDEA: USDOC, 2004).

Claim 2: For students with disabilities, however, low inclusion rates in general education classes have not resulted in equitable outcomes.

Claim 3: The history of special education is one of inequitable educational access, influenced by misunderstandings, superstitions, inappropriate care, bias, and prejudices, with higher rates noted for underrepresented minority students.

Claim 4: Individuals with Disabilities Education Act (IDEA) provided broad mandates, including mechanisms for identifying and counting students, thereby providing accurate funding and disbursements.

Claim 5: IDEA set forth evaluation and eligibility determination guidelines, the requirement of parental input, due process procedures, and the novel term "least restrictive environment" as a measure for inclusion.

Claim 6: A principal's leadership is a powerful predictor of the school's ability to provide appropriate environments and effective services for students with disabilities.

Claim 7: Principals typically lack a program training background, professional development, or practical experience, in the field of students with disabilities.

Claim 8: School principals, responsible for improving outcomes for *all* students, have reported feeling poorly prepared – through inadequate training, lack of sufficient coursework, and lack of field experience in special education.

Claim 9: Research specifically indicates that principals require job-embedded learning opportunities, through on-site professional development, to guarantee student-centered practices supporting students with disabilities.

Claim 10: While research identifies necessary principal competencies, no research exists on *how* those competencies manifest as inclusive practices and how principals obtain those competencies on-the-job.

The above line of claims may guide and order the Literature Review. The model above reveals the logical move from the broad problem (appropriate education for *all*) to the specific research focus (school principals need on-the-job competencies to support students with disabilities in general education classrooms). Expanding the claims helped the student write this key chapter.

Practices that help with creating a set of arguments

1. **Write:** For your project, create a similar set of logical claims. What is the underlying logic of this line of claims?

2. **Place** your studies: Given your set of claims, what articles would you discuss under each claim?

3. **Write a paragraph** that depicts the context of your study, citing key research.

4. **Write** a provisional opening roadmap that anticipates the logical progression of the chapter.

Refining your claims into an outline, with subpoints

Your set of claims can underpin an outline, which then is continuously revised and refined. When you add to your research, your outline may generate new causes or contributing events. Further, your sub-headings may grow. In the example below, which has several layers of subordinate points, the writer began with low U.S. k-12 math achievement and failed interventions, especially for middle school students of color (SOC). When he got to causes, he identified how stereotype threat (ST) affects math achievement. Under this sub-heading, his outline further divided into various theories of stereotype threat, its effects, and proposed interventions. The interventions subdivided further, narrowing to neuroscience-based interventions (very few), which lack both trainings and assessment – creating a gap.

Here is what that refined logic outline looked like.

The achievement gap in math for SOC

I. Context:

    A. National, state, and district statistics reveal an achievement gap for SOC.

    B. National interventions (e.g. No Child Left Behind) improved overall scores, but the gap remained.

    C. Manifestations of the problem include low attendance, low engagement, and low math scores.

    D. Well-researched interventions that have not fixed the problem include:

        1. Mentoring

        2. Professional development

        3. After-school programs

II. Causes of low math scores for SOC are far-reaching and pervasive.

    A. Socio-economic

    B. Systemic racism

    C. ST

        1. Definitions and theories of ST

        2. ST's negative effect on math achievement

        3. Mitigation measures for ST

            a. Mindset and other interventions, but they lack empirical data

            b. Changing mindset by applying theories of neuroplasticity – promising theory

            c. Some evidence of improved math engagement, but few practices from theory

            d. Gap: need for training in and assessment of anti-ST practices for teaching math

The above outline indicates an argument from broad problem, to specific manifestation, to the gap in the research. It also indicates the layers of subpoints that will help place the literature.

Practices: refining your outline

1. **Outline:** Using the above model, write a more detailed outline of the arguments for your study.

2. **Refine the outline:** Subdivide those arguments still further into sub-points, and reference appropriate articles.

3. **Identify** a place in your outline where you identify solutions (or new theories). Under each add a few key studies. Is there a gap in the research? If so, **explain.**

In sum

With help from outlining, you can develop a project plan to guide your reading. You then refine your outline by creating additional sub-headings, especially concerning studies close to your own. In the above example, the student saw mindset as close to stereotype threat, garnering considerable attention in the literature but little empirical data. He proposed collecting quantitative and qualitative data on his neuroscience-based middle school math intervention, one that he created, which he hypothesized would activate a growth mindset. This gap in the research on practice left room for him to propose his own project.

To recap: An outline helps you anticipate and direct your Literature Review search. You can start with your existing arguments and sub-arguments, then fill in with the studies you already have, and then direct a new search. You continually ask yourself, what do I still need? This early thinking and writing save you considerable time and lessen the temptation to follow those wayward studies down the rabbit hole.

Part 2: Stepping back and reflecting on your literature

Overview

With a detailed outline as a logic guide, you can return to your search. What follows describes a process – the outline generates a search, but the search turns up studies that may change the outline. Keep in mind that you will continue to locate, review, and write about studies, right up until you submit your finished dissertation. However, key activities are important as you go forward from your outline.

Reflecting is key

New studies surface all the time, so you need to keep updating and reflecting on what you have. You can rethink and rewrite the context that bears on your study – a natural place to start. But If you get stuck with your opening, postpone working on it until later. This is not the place to get stuck. Move on, whenever you find yourself going down the rabbit hole of too much reading.

A Literature Review *combines* studies, so reflect on *relationships* – how do key researchers build on each other's work and cite each other? How has the research developed? How do key studies support or challenge each other? Take some time to reflect here.

Practices for reflecting on the literature

1. **Reflect and write:** What do you think are the most telling national (or state or district) studies you could use as context? Consolidate them into a short paragraph.

2. **Write to see connections:** For each part of your argument, what relationships do you see among the key studies? Do researchers confirm/build on each other's work?

3. **Write an analysis:** Where you narrow, what 3–5 studies are most like your own? How do they help you argue for your study? Write a paragraph consolidating these studies.

4. **Take notes:** For those studies closest to your own, what researcher names keep reappearing? What seems to be the history of their research?

5. **Take additional notes:** What contrary evidence have you uncovered, if any? How is this evidence best understood?

6. **Refine:** Identify any significant new studies to place under the headings and sub-headings, to guide your drafting.

7. **Rewrite** your outline, noting where you still need to fill in more literature.

Adding a conceptual framework

Through reading and outlining, you reach a point where you have key claims and relevant studies for your project. You have a path forward. However, there is likely a central addition to make to your outline: the theories that comprise *the conceptual framework* that undergirds your study.

A conceptual framework consists of the theories you combine to explain your research assumptions. While you may have started with a theory, for instance, neuroplasticity (a unique underpinning for k-12 math instruction), the conceptual framework often develops as you review the literature and refine your study. For instance, the proposed k-12 middle school math intervention required theories of engagement, stereotype threat, mindset, and finally neuroscience. You will need to make explicit your framework and to argue for why it applies. This description typically comes at the end of the

Literature Review, but it may also appear at the beginning. You might try it in either place and see how it fits into your outline.

Practice: integrating a conceptual framework into the outline

Write a refined, more nuanced outline of the literature on your problem that includes your conceptual framework.

In sum

Before drafting this critical chapter, you need to pre-write extensively (outline, reflect, add, outline again). Using your initial outline from your Problem Statement, you expand it by adding research that strengthens your argument; then you refine the outline. As you go, you take time to reflect on the studies you have, the new ones you are collecting, and the overall arguments they support. As noted, a final piece is likely needed – where you detail the conceptual framework – the theories that likely govern the key studies you have found and your own proposed work. These typically emerge from your research – they are the theories that researchers already use and that you will naturally build into your own study. But it helps to place the theories in your refined outline, before setting out to draft this chapter.

Part 3: Drafting your literature review

Overview

The first draft of your Literature Review will likely appear incomplete, as it requires synthesizing many lines of research. Assume a complex process of writing, review, additions, and reworking. But once you put thoughts into sentences, that act spawns more thoughts, more connections, and the sentences become more sentences. Don't worry about getting it right – try to get a flow of ideas going. What follows are some considerations about writing processes. Later comes some practical advice on fleshing out, and also deleting, sources you need (or don't).

Initial drafting of the literature review

Draft as much of this chapter as you can by following your outline, pushing ahead without worrying about error, concentrating on convincing your reader through argument and evidence, and using what you know from your reading, not what you don't know, to move forward. Put apprehension behind and plunge in.

Practices to keep you pushing to complete a first draft

1. With your refined outline as guide, **quick-write** (without looking back) a paragraph that serves the reader as a roadmap through the arguments you will present. Don't worry about accuracy or correctness. This roadmap will later get rewritten and better predict for readers what is to come. But at this stage, it prompts the flow of sentences and keeps you on track. Once you have this roadmap in writing, use it as a prompt for further writing. Expect to revise the roadmap various times through the course of your dissertation work.

2. **Write in a new Word file** the whole first section – the Introduction, the context of your problem, the problem itself. Use your outline for guidance with main points and supportive studies. Detail the most salient statistics or vivid details depicting the problem. Make the case as strong as you can, but do not overload the reader with overlapping evidence.

3. Next, **continue writing in your Word file** any section in your outline that seems clearest to you. You may want to work backward and compose the section on the studies most closely related to your own. Or you may want to draft a section in the middle of your Literature Review.

4. **Draft** the conceptual framework, as these theories underpin your study.

5. **Write in your Word document** the rest of the sections, from your outline.

6. **Take notes to yourself as you go:** Identify places that seem to lack sufficient evidence. Leave placeholder notes for yourself to attend to later. Do not allow yourself to worry about the ragged nature of this first draft. Words on the page are what count.

Reading aloud your initial draft

Reread your draft. Feel free to add or change pieces as you revise, as rewriting can be done either in small pieces or on the work as a whole. But sometimes it is helpful to read a piece aloud. You hear the thoughts on the page. This practice often triggers thought in a different way than rereading silently.

Practices

1. Read aloud your initial draft of your Literature Review. **Mark on this draft** where it seems compelling and where it feels sketchy. **Write in your journal:** What makes any strong section sound so compelling? Where do you feel the writing needs work?

2. **Ask** a colleague to read and comment on the draft. **Take notes in your journal:** What suggestions seem most helpful?

3. **Write in your journal a revision plan:** What will you do to strengthen the argument?

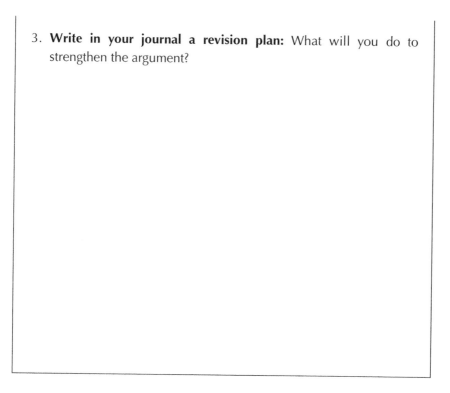

Using your annotated bibliography to flesh out the draft

You have diverse materials to extend this Literature Review draft. Take another look at your annotated bibliography to help with detailing this chapter. The annotations help you decide which studies pertain. The annotations not only capture study details but also typically indicate the strength of a study's findings. Choose strong studies, reread your annotations for important details, and, using practices below, **build the details into your Word document**. The annotations may also reveal convergence – where groups of studies together argue for your study.

Practices using annotations

1. **Write notes in your journal:** What key argument needs to be enhanced by selecting study details from your annotated bibliography? What are those details?

2. **Review:** Have you overlooked a few key studies you annotated much earlier? Which might you use?

3. **Review and edit:** How are you connecting the studies? **Make notes in your journal** about where you need connections. In your Word document, sharpen weak connections to support your point.

4. **Revise a section of your Word document**, including more of your annotations. Write in placeholders where you still need to fill in study evidence.

In sum

The advice for writing the first draft of your Literature Review is to write without worry. It is a process. You will revise. And you have multiple sources and prewriting materials to draw from. Using your outline, write about what you have without hesitation. Try to get the initial draft out fairly quickly, not stopping to edit. Then read aloud your initial draft. New directions may surface, but also new assessments. As the next section suggests, you may find you need to let some sources go. Not all of your initial writing will stay. But trust that more and better writing will take its place. This is a learning process, not a race to the finish.

Part 4: Reviewing – letting some sources (and writing) go

Overview

While it takes hard work to find sources, new arguments may change what you need. Some articles, seemingly helpful, may become less relevant. As one example, your research questions may change. For another, you may need to cut back on too much background. Also likely, you may find more targeted, credible studies. As a result, you may need to let some of the old sources and arguments go.

It is difficult to let go of any writing. But dissertation writers find that by reassessing their sources, they sharpen how they see their work. With that clarity comes an easier flow of new writing. Once again: The writing propels the thought, and the thought the writing. You need words on the page but also words off the page, to clear the decks. This process begins early.

Fortunately, students become astute in assessing relevance. They may rewrite sections of the Literature Review even after the data have been collected and the findings written. Below are some practices to review your sources.

Reassessing your sources

Periodically, you reassess your sources for relevance, credibility, and persuasiveness. You may need to resign some to the dustbin (in a reserve file). The following assessment guide may help:

- **Assessing use:** As noted earlier, the source needs to be published by a credible outlet: a well-respected journal in the field or a key publisher of academic work; it is recent, peer-reviewed, and often cited.
- **Assessing relevance:** The study's research question or purpose is closely tied to an argument you are making.
- **Assessing place in the field:** The source's own Literature Review looks substantial and relates to other studies you are citing.

- **Assessing persuasiveness:** The scope, collected data, and analysis look persuasive.
- **Assessing your need:** It is foundational, referenced by your other studies, and/or pivotal to your argument. It is the strongest of several similar studies.

Practices for reviewing for need

1. **Review** your sources. What sources seem unnecessary or circumscribed? **List** a few here that you question.

2. **Rewrite** a paragraph that seems overly general. Use new data from more targeted sources. Add commentary, if needed.

3. **Reconsider and note:** What kind of evidence could heighten the argument in a particular section? What new data sources do you plan to investigate? **Make notes** here.

4. **Reconsider:** What contrary or moderating evidence has surfaced (if any)? **Comment here.**

In-text citing (how not to overdo it)

Maybe you don't need duplicative sources. The problem of unnecessary sources can be seen in the writing below, where the writer seems to have too much of a good thing:

> Lack of teacher preparation has been linked to higher levels of teacher attrition (Betts, Rueben, & Dannenberg, 2000; Carver-Thomas & Darling-Hammond, 2017b; Zhang & Zeller, 2016), and lower student achievement scores (Carver-Thomas & Darling-Hammond, 2017a; Fetler, 1999; Goe, 2002). With teacher quality being the most critical in-school factor influencing student achievement (Rivkin, Hanushek, & Kain, 2001; Sanders & Rivers, 1996; Wright, Horn, & Sanders, 1997), it is vital for students to be taught by well-prepared, high-quality teachers.

There are too many sources cited for each general statement. The writer can remove some. Reminder: As you are the developing expert, you decide which studies are essential. Keep in mind that you don't need to be exhaustive.

Practices

1. Eliminate all but one or two cited studies per claim in the above excerpt, even without knowing their content. **Reflect in your journal:** How did you decide? How is the reading of the two sentences improved?

2. **Rewrite** some sentences you have written where too many citations block flow.

In sum

You continually reassess your sources and thus your argument. This practice teaches you the critical skills you need as a researcher. And the more you research and rewrite to clarify your argument, the less precious become the words you use. This critical stance helps you prioritize key studies, persuade more forcefully, and show concern for readers by not citing everything you have found. When writers overload readers by using too many citations, they actually weaken their reader's understanding of the very points being stressed.

Part 5: Creating a second draft of the Literature Review

Overview

Having a first draft written, you will find redrafting this chapter more straightforward. You have developed arguments, created and used an outline, and reassessed the case you are making. Further, you have included details from your annotated bibliography to give depth to the cited studies. In addition, you have substituted more credible studies for weaker, off-target ones, and used placeholders for where you need to include more literature. It is time to write a second full draft despite unfinished spots.

Reviewing how you open

Openings carry special weight. Your opening sets the scene and provides an entry point for your reader. Consider a new, more engaging way in, one that sketches for your reader the larger picture (concerns, studies, history, telling example) in which your study will be enacted. Here, you suggest the breadth of knowledge that bears on your study. Also, make sure your roadmap predicts where you are going.

Practices for revising the opening

1. In your journal, **brainstorm** different openings, each with a different context. Give yourself some options.

2. **In your journal, take notes on how to rewrite and extend** your introductory roadmap. **Note** where you need connectors as to how the sections relate.

3. **In your Word document**, rewrite these sections to make sure the opening and roadmap fit and predict what follows. Reread and revise your draft for consistency.

Reviewing arguments for content

Not all arguments are equally persuasive. And you can't always see where your argument is flagging. But before you ask others to read your redrafted Literature Review, put your work aside for a few days, and come back to it for a review. You may find that you are reading it afresh, as if you were a new reader.

Practices

1. After a few days, review your arguments for content. **Revise** key places in your Word document for additional content.
2. **In your journal, list** next steps, including revisions to places where you have placeholders.

3. Reread the draft again as a critical reader would. **Identify** where you think readers might ask questions or need more evidence.

4. **Rewrite** pieces of your Word document in response to that rereading through the eyes of outside readers.

Signposting before sharing

Another important activity before you share your Literature Review draft with others is to signpost your sections accurately – to make it easier for readers to follow. The biggest signposts are your headers and sub-headers. Review again what you have. As a reminder, with headers you title larger sections; subtitles allow you to divide them into smaller sections. This titling previews for readers what the piece of writing contains (avoid single word titles)– so you can create reader expectations, then appease them, increasing reader receptiveness.

Practices

1. **Add or rewrite** headers to your Word document, to better guide your readers.
2. Where might sub-headers help? **Add** these to any long stretch of writing.
3. **Check:** Does the writing under the headers and sub-headers stay with that topic? Are there places where you might be veering off-topic? Review the connection between these titles and the text that falls under them. **Revise** where needed.

Topic sentences: a checkpoint for logic

Before sending to a reviewer or your Chair, look for how your paragraphs connect. Pay attention to your topic sentences, to make sure they form bridges that hold this chapter together. The first sentence of each paragraph typically makes the claim for that section, and what follows provides the evidence. These topic sentences should link together. A key test is to write all the topic sentences alone, as a series; the series should communicate the logic of the study. Make sure they work as transitions or bridges so that readers follow your logic. You want to show how the main point of one paragraph relates to the main point of next paragraph. You can check to see if you are missing any bridges.

Practices

1. **In your journal, list** (in the order that they appear) the topic sentences of each of your paragraphs of your Literature Review.

2. **Take notes:** Do you see any gaps or lack of connections in the above topic sentences? If so, rewrite those sentences to bridge ideas.

3. **Reflect in your journal:** Is there another order that would make more sense? Or does this order work the best? Why?

4. **Reread yet another time.**

Working with your Chair (sending this chapter out for review)

After this extensive work, you need fresh eyes. Your draft needs to be fully reviewed. It is a complex piece of work, so first ask a colleague to review your chapter; take notes on their response. If you receive positive feedback, send your full draft to your Chair for feedback.

Some notes on exchanges with your Chair: You will likely have submitted questions, plans, or partial drafts to your Chair before this key juncture. However, each student works out a different arrangement for preliminary guidance. The suggestion here is that you establish with your Chair key benchmarks for submissions. You do not want to flood your Chair with Literature Review drafts (the Chair will become tired, inured, less effective). But you also don't want to move in wrong directions. It is important to have shared an outline and asked for additional topics and readings, to preclude concerns at your Preliminary Orals. And you likely want to set up doable goals along the way, to keep you directed.

Have a conversation with your Chair about how submissions and feedback would work best – whether you can calendar meetings periodically, how much lead time the Chair needs for reading, how much back and forth is likely between written responses. Again, be sure to ask to record all meetings.

Practices

1. **Write in your journal** some questions for your Chair.

2. **Record and take notes** on what your Chair suggests. After the meeting or response, **write in your journal**: What is the major concern? Do you feel you understand the feedback?

3. **Respond** to the feedback with appreciation and any further questions.
4. **Rewrite** the Word document, based on the feedback. Be prepared for further revisions. Be pleased if the commentary is extensive: You are on your way.

Chapter summary

The Literature Review remains fluid throughout your study and throughout the writing of your dissertation. Writing, reevaluating, and rewriting it are essential practices in dissertation work. However, practices such as writing claims, outlining, reassessing sources, connecting sources, and sharing plans and drafts with your Chair will smooth out the process. You continue to work on the Literature Review as you move forward, possibly adding and removing pieces. You will come back to it again, when you write your Discussion chapter: In that chapter, you will likely discuss how your new findings relate to these preexisting studies – confirming, adding to, or contradicting them. At this stage, however, creating a strong initial set of research-based arguments confirms the work you are proposing. Of additional help, reading these studies has likely generated ideas about your Methodology, the subject of the next chapter.

Writing the Methodology

Your methods are central to the credibility of your study. You likely began thinking about how you would do your study from the moment you chose your topic. While your Chair may have cautioned, *do not to jump to methods before you define the problem*, it is hard to keep from imagining yourself actually doing the study – where it would be held, who would be involved, what you would ask, and what you want to find out. So first off, curb that enthusiasm – a tad: Your Chair is right. *Your methods follow your research questions, which come from exploring your problem (not promoting your solution)*. You don't want a disjunction between research questions and the data you gather. That would send you back to the drawing board.

What follows extends some of the earlier advice on methods for your Problem Statement. You need the same elements, only argued (explained and supported) more fully. You will also add new sections – on data analysis, credibility, ethical considerations, and positionality. These pieces come together to convince readers that you have a viable, credible study.

Part 1: Revising your research questions

Overview

The mantra of this section is, once again, that *your research questions change*. You need to maintain balance, through all the uncertainty. John Dewey, in *How We Think* (1910/1971), puts the paradox well: The researcher "needs to maintain the state of doubt and to carry on

DOI: 10.4324/9781003519904-4

systematic and protracted inquiry" (p. 3). Here, Dewey notes that systematic *belief* over years is coupled with systematic *doubt* – a continued ambiguity. In sustained inquiry, change is a given.

It helps to write a preliminary list of possible research questions, knowing that some overlap, some are too broad, and some are irrelevant; even the best one or two will still evolve, up to the Preliminary Orals. Then, the questions likely evolve again. In rare cases, the questions change after the data have been collected and analyzed: The student and Chair realize that the analysis answers a different but equally significant question: Better to revise the question than to scuttle the study.

Why revision is so important

Every word in a research question matters. Each question implies a kind of data and an approach to analyzing those data; each question also limits the kind of data that can be used. Your questions typically evolve by becoming more precise and limiting.

Practice

Write: Create three possible research questions. Then write some unexpected responses you might get from each question. What words need changing to better govern responses?

Revising your questions: limiting the data you collect

You will need to pinpoint the concrete data you want to collect to answer each question. Without such forethought, the questions and the data may not align. Take, for example, a research question in the mixed-methods study that targeted middle school math students: It asked whether or not their *liking of* math improved after a six-week anti-stereotype threat intervention. The quantitative data collected on improved *liking* did not answer the research question of whether the intervention reduced stereotype threat. The intervention had improved measures of math achievement, but it turns out that *liking* was unrelated. Students did not like math any better after the six weeks (what middle school students would?). But on other measures – such as effort, engagement, and self-appraisal of ability – students showed reduced stereotype threat. So not *liking* math proved a poor indicator of reduced threat.

Practices for using questions to circumscribe data

Reflect in your journal: What are the key words in each of your proposed research questions? What does each word imply about the kind of data you can use? Why might those data not answer your research question?

Write: Take a research question, and rewrite it to limit the study to data that will explicitly answer the question.

Adding to your research questions

Sometimes you need to add a question, not just rework one. The student researcher above soon saw he needed to gather very specific qualitative data on how teachers perceived students' reaction to the intervention. So, he added, *what do teachers perceive to be students' changes in engagement, including class attendance, turning work in on time, completing work, and asking questions.* He had noted that stereotype threat is typically measured in the literature as engagement. The study ended up with a convergence of qualitative and quantitative data indicating that the intervention did reduce stereotype threat.

Practices

1. **Jot down:** What additional research questions or sub-questions could generate important data?

2. **Evaluate:** Which of the questions you have could be overarching research questions, and which could be interview, focus group, or survey questions? Why?

Revising your questions: how will your study be used and by whom?

In addition to ensuring a tight fit between research questions and data collected, you want your study to mean something to groups of readers. By envisioning how your study could be used and by whom, you can rethink your questions.

Practices to revise questions to reflect the study's use

1. Use your journal to **reflect:** Who do you think could use the findings from your study? Explain.

2. **Brainstorm and give examples:** How would they use the findings?

3. **Reflect:** Does thinking about how people might use your study's data make you rethink your research questions? Explain.

4. **Revise:** Rewrite several of your research questions, or add a question that you think might make your study be of wider use.

Revising your questions: how can you ensure your study's contribution?

Some students create research questions to which they already know the answer. They are looking to confirm what they already know, perhaps adding only a new population or site. Such a study will not likely contribute much. Rather, research questions need to genuinely probe what we don't know and what we sense to be important to know.

Practices to revise questions, in light of the study's contribution

1. **Envision and Write:** What is the source of your choice of questions? What do you *genuinely not know* that you think your study can uncover?

2. **Describe:** What personal experiences, if any, have generated your questions? How will answers to this question make a difference to others?

3. **Reflect on the literature:** If you are interested in understanding a well-researched phenomenon, such as gender bias in science, technology, engineering, and mathematics, what question will go beyond what we already know?

4. **Rewrite:** Add a question to better generate potential new knowledge.

In sum

To underscore: Your research questions change throughout this dissertation process. Reasons vary, from issues of clarity and alignment, to needing to limit or add data, to considerations of use, to ensuring the study's contribution. Most important is that you can use your questions to guide the processes of your study – through your selection of design, sites and participants, data collection and analysis, and presentation of findings and conclusions.

Part 2: Reasons behind your design

Overview

The design is your approach – qualitative, quantitative, or mixed. A qualitative study asks open-ended questions about perceptions, processes, experiences, reflections, narratives, and contexts; a quantitative study uses pre-determined ratings, effects, measurements, usage, scores, and degree of approval – to fit data along a spectrum. A mixed-methods study uses both, for different purposes. Your research questions typically imply a design, the needed overall approach.

Students often think that the design of a study is a matter of personal choice. They *prefer* a qualitative or a quantitative study (or mixed methods), based on their background or experience. In this thinking, they misconstrue. The design of a study depends on the kind of data that can answer the research questions, the strength of the rationale for that approach over some other approach, and the Chair's recommendations.

Identifying your predilections

First, let's probe some of your preferences: Many students immediately think of doing either a quantitative or a qualitative study. It is important to examine such set ideas before jumping to a design that may not fit your study goals. Try to remain open to other approaches than the one you anticipate using.

Practices

1. **Recollect:** What approach have you always anticipated using (qualitative, quantitative, or mixed?)? Why that approach?

2. **Reflect and envision in your journal:** Have you considered some of the advantages of a different approach? What might those be? What are the disadvantages?

3. **Assess arguments, in notes:** What arguments could readers present for a different study design? What worries you about this alternative design?

4. **Write to persuade:** Explain to a skeptical reader why you have chosen your design. Make sure you reference the anticipated research questions and the goals and use of the study.

Mindset

You may be coming to your study with a fixed mindset that you are skilled at only one study approach. Before settling on the design, try to understand where your views come from so that discussions with your Chair can be objective.

Practices

1. **Reflect in writing:** What in your own experience makes you resist or lean toward a particular design?

2. **Reflect:** Try envisioning a design different from what you anticipated. What could you learn from that different design?

3. **Argue the opposite:** Using the above, write an argument for a different kind of design, to better understand alternatives.

Justifying your design objectively

By holding personal preference in abeyance, you can concentrate on constructing the argument for your design. This objectivity is especially important in your Preliminary Orals, where you may be questioned about your choices. Read several methods books or sections of books on design, where methodologists discuss the reasons behind a particular approach.

Practices

1. **Research and Write:** What is the strongest argument that methodologists might make for your design? Find a key quote and explain how it applies to your study.

2. **Research and Write:** Looking through these methods texts, did you come across a credible argument for another design? If so, explain its benefit.

3. **Write to persuade:** In your journal, fully defend your choice of design by also recognizing the benefits/disadvantages of an alternate design. How does your chosen design best fit your research questions?

> ## In sum
>
> *In your draft, the design section typically follows the research questions but often precedes them in your thinking, as students often come to their research with leanings toward a specific kind of study. What matters in the end is that (1) the study design matches the research questions, (2) the rationale for both is objective and well argued, and (3) the data collected will be credible and significant.*

Part 3: Rationale for data collection methods

Overview

Your rationale for your list of data collection methods develops from your research questions and design. You want the right kind of data (given your choices and access). And you want enough data to generate significant findings. But you don't want to collect so much data that you become swamped in it: Keep in mind that some sources are much more relevant than others. Also keep in mind that when you write up findings, you will need to do *data reduction*, limiting what you write about. If you have too many data sources and have spawned reams of data, your data reduction, analysis, and writing processes will be much more difficult.

Self-questioning

Simple questions arise: Why interviews and focus groups, if both come from the same participants? Why not observations and interviews, given that observations come from a different source? Do you need documents to throw light on (and possibly contradict) interview responses? If the study is mostly documents, how can you confirm (triangulate) from another source? A key question may arise if a student proposes sending a survey form to a large institutional email list – only to identify a small number of potential interviewees: Why not use that broad survey, with its high numbers, to gather key data on a research question? Could you add several open-ended questions, still keeping the study qualitative? Overall, ask what weaknesses or biases each data source might produce that could require some confirmation.

It is understandable that some students may want to avoid the messiness of mixed methods. Yet, if a student has wide access for a survey, and a likely high response rate, a broad survey's results (e.g. in rates, scores, percentages) would heighten credibility of a purely qualitative study, promoting needed breadth. In one instance, a study of charter schools' treatment of Emotional Disturbance, in response to a California policy change, was strengthened when the writer combined results from a charter school survey with data from in-depth interviews.

Practices for self-questioning

1. **Write:** List in your journal the data sources you think most essential to your study. Prioritize them.

2. **Take notes:** What information will each data source provide?

3. **Take notes:** What biases might evolve from using only one source for your data collection? What is the most likely confirming or contradicting source that might be needed?

4. **Reflect:** Are you choosing your data source because of convenience? What bias might ensue? How can you overcome difficulties using a different data source method?

Specifying the kind of data you will collect

You need to be explicit about what you will collect. For each data collection method, provide readers with *units of observation* – examples of the kind of empirical data that will serve to answer your questions.

Practices to get you thinking about specifics

1. **Create a Units of Observation table**. The table identifies concrete observable data in one column and aligns each with a specific research question in another column.

2. **Describe:** How will analyzing these data answer the research questions?

3. **Identify** new Units of Observation that may further help you answer your research questions. Explain what each will tell you.

Writing and rewriting your rationale

Once you have selected your data collection methods, with justifications, and detailed the kind of data you will collect (including your survey and protocol questions), you need to have them approved by your Chair.

Don't wait until Preliminary Orals. Other committee members may find weaknesses in your justification and then suggest data sources and protocols that you have not anticipated.

Practice in writing a rationale for your data

1. **Write in your journal:** In a paragraph or two, compose a compelling rationale for the data you will collect, why those data sources over other sources, and how those data will answer your research questions.

2. **Write:** A preliminary interview or survey protocol for one of your sources.

3. **Take notes**: After piloting the set of questions, what changes did the responses indicate that you need to make?

4. **Rewrite** in a Word document the key early parts of this chapter – your design and data collection methods and rationale, along with your revised protocol questions – to submit to your Chair.

In sum

Your data collection methods, like your research questions, undergo scrutiny and revision. You need a tight connection between research questions, design, and data collection. Keep an open mind about how you will best obtain the data. And be realistic about your access to that data, as well as any issues of recruitment you can anticipate. If you are solely analyzing existing data, you still need to justify that data source, how you will use it, and your access to it.

Part 4: Site and participants/subjects

Overview

You choose your site and participants/subjects based on the likelihood of obtaining credible data. Reviewers will be concerned with too much of a convenience factor, or with any bias these choices might reveal. You will also need to clarify your access and means of recruiting your subjects or participants.

Rationale for your site(s)

In choosing your site(s), you convince readers that your choices embody the problem investigated. For instance, a study of the leadership involved in managing community college enrollment loss required the student to choose a community college district revealing decreased enrollment. However, a district with multiple colleges might balance the shortfalls of one college against increases at others. So, the researcher chose *single-college* districts across Southern California. This was a valid rationale.

Practices

1. **Consider and write:** What are your key criteria for choosing your site(s)? Explain why.

2. **Write a persuasive entry:** How does your site(s) meet the criteria? Also, if too wide a swath of sites fit those criteria, how would you narrow the criteria?

3. **Write notes to preclude objections:** What concerns might readers have with your choice of site(s)? How would you address those concerns?

Rationale for your choice of participants

You also need criteria for selecting your participants or subjects. These criteria emerge from your problem and your research questions. However, these criteria may also require considerable site-based knowledge: Ask yourself: Who are these participants? What do they do at their site that is essential to the study? How do I locate them? How will I recruit them? Given a unique study, the criteria may have to be flexible. And getting your sample may involve a lot of preparatory work.

For the qualitative study of enrollment management in single-campus community colleges, the researcher needed participants with knowledge of, and leadership in, enrollment management. Such individuals varied considerably at each site. Their job titles showed a significant spread, including district manager, faculty leader, classified staff leader, and member of an enrollment management committee.

Given such a difference in job titles, the researcher needed underlying *criteria*, and reasons for including faculty and classified staff leaders in the sample. Working against titles as criteria, the student emphasized participants' *knowledge and role in governance:* Because all these different participants were involved in college participatory governance, they met the criteria of knowledge and leadership.

Practices

1. **Thinking in advance:** What criteria do you anticipate using to select your participants or subjects? Why those criteria? **Jot notes** in your journal.

2. **Take notes:** What benefits or problems could accrue if you limited your sample more? If you expanded it more?

3. **Reflect:** What might be readers' most significant critique of your criteria?

4. **Write** a paragraph or more detailing your sample selection method.

Access and recruitment

Site access and participant recruitment may seem easy. You simply ask people for their cooperation. However, access to both site and to data can be problematic. Site administrators may be loath to support studies that investigate a problem they want to work on themselves, with little publicity. Potential participants may not want a time commitment. Potential survey respondents may not even take the time to fill out an extensive questionnaire. You will need a plan to overcome these barriers.

Practices

1. **Outline** in your journal a memorandum of understanding letter to secure from a site leader – guaranteeing you access to their site.

2. **Write** an access plan for your committee to see: who you contacted, what agreements were made, how you addressed any barriers.

3. **Write:** For a survey, explain: What heads of organizations did you contact to obtain help in response rates? Also, explain: What help will they provide? What will you do if the response rate is low?

4. **Write** a recruitment plan for your committee to see, one that includes how many participants or subjects you anticipate, how you will contact them, what assurances you will give them, what incentives you will provide for their participation, and how you will adjust if you get fewer participants or subjects than you need.

In sum

Your site and sample may seem uncomplicated choices, but they require much thought and anticipation. You need criteria, arguments that support those criteria, anticipation of barriers and roadblocks, and much preparatory work. Your choices can involve very creative decision-making. But they also need planning, scrutiny, and good judgment.

Part 5: Plan for analyzing the data

Overview

A quantitative study already has its plan locked in for the kind of data to be collected and the method chosen for analyzing those data. Usually, these methods involve some data analysis tool, already specified, such as SPSS (Statistical Package for the Social Sciences). The plan is typically created with the Chair, and is in place early in the process, at the proposal stage. For a qualitative study, the plan is more hypothetical. The researcher does not know what kind of data will surface. Still, you need to specify what kind of analysis you intend to do and how you will do it.

Reassuring your readers

Key to a data analysis plan is reassuring one's committee that your processes are credible, given your research questions. For a quantitative study, the questionnaire itself, and the description of why those questions, serves to convince readers of credibility. You likely need to pilot the questions so that you can assure readers that the questions measure what you say they do (the measures are valid). For qualitative studies, detailing the processes reinforces credibility. For instance, details might include that you will read and reread the data, coding it and recoding it, for accuracy. You might also state that you are employing an additional coder to eliminate bias. Other details might pinpoint different kinds of coding: descriptive coding, simultaneous coding, coding for elements of a theory, or coding for emerging themes. (These are described in methods books and online sites.)

While readers understand the hypothetical nature of qualitative plans for analysis, they also want assurances that you have thought through options and have plans and expertise to work with the data you collect.

Practices

1. **Write in your journal** an initial plan for analyzing your data, for a quantitative, qualitative, or mixed-methods study, that reassures readers of your concern for credibility. Provide details.

2. **Create an initial list** of all of the processes you will engage in, including any data analysis tool, and/or how you will code and recode the data – leading to emergent themes or some other analytic frame.

3. **Write** a paragraph in which you summarize all that you will do to make your processes credible.

Weighing specific kinds of data analysis methods

You will need a good grasp of the methods of data analysis that exist. As noted, quantitative researchers need these plans upfront and have likely taken courses that have schooled them in the tools available to them. Qualitative researchers need more exposure to kinds of analysis. Content analysis, discourse analysis, and narrative analysis are just a few of the standard analysis methods, once coding is done. Your Chair will be helpful in guiding you. But you will need to put the rationale in your own words.

Practices

1. **Write to anticipate:** After consulting with your Chair, what standard data analysis method will you use, if any? Explain why.

2. **Write:** What adjustments to that method, if any, do you anticipate using? Why?

3. **Write to envision:** Given your choice of analysis methods, write a paragraph in your journal arguing for your choice of methods. Be explicit about the sequence of actions you will take.

In sum

Readers, most specifically your committee members, need assurance that your choice of data analysis methods fits your data, your objectives, and your research questions. The clearer you make the processes and the rationale, the more convincing your study will be. Your Chair's advice is critical here.

Part 6: Study credibility and trustworthiness; validity and reliability

Overview

Once the study is complete, you need to rewrite your plan to state what you actually did. A qualitative study needs to describe how it *achieved credibility* (the findings are true and accurate) because credibility is central to its *trustworthiness*. Credibility is confirmed through using multiple sources, long engagement with the data, member checks, and continued observation; it also needs to ensure against reactivity, where participants respond differently from how they actually feel and give a socially prompted or desired response. A quantitative study needs to describe how it achieved *validity* (the instrument measures what it is supposed to) and *reliability* (the results are consistent, when one repeats the study). Beyond their initial planning, dissertation writers need to explain how they ensured the quality of their findings. For final submission, you complete a separate, detailed section under Methods to address these concerns.

Confirming credibility

A foundational strategy to build credibility in qualitative work, and thus create trustworthiness, involves removing perceived risks or benefits for particular responses. You can assure respondents of the need for an honest report and also that they will be protected from harm through anonymity. Another strategy, noted above, is to specify multiple data sources (triangulating data): When you later analyze an array of data and determine that different sources (e.g. district administrators and teachers) have similar reports, you strengthen credibility. Further, you can check and recheck your write-up of participants' responses to avoid researcher bias, given that your background may lean toward one kind of interpretation. Other planning strategies that confirm credibility include field testing protocols and using standard coding procedures. You can also stress that you will engage for long periods with your data and provide rich descriptions to support findings. Given such considerations, you need to record the measures you actually take. When you detail such strategies, you persuade readers of the study's credibility.

Practices for credibility, thus confirming trustworthiness

1. **Write to sharpen credibility:** What alternate sources of data could confirm or disconfirm your reports? If you avoided using them, explain why.

2. **Write to remind yourself:** How will you recheck with participants (*members' checks*) to see if you are accurately reporting their words or actions? Explain.

3. **Practice describing:** Provide a rich description of one participant's observed behavior or interview response. What in that description increases the credibility of your finding?

4. **Detail**: How did you guard against participant reactivity?

Further confirming trustworthiness

You further confirm trustworthiness by detailing how you derived your findings from your data. Readers need concrete details on each step – from data collection, to coding, to findings – so that other researchers can review processes and also perform similar studies. This is called an *audit trail*, which records the research process, going back as far as identifying a problem and creating research questions, to deriving findings and conclusions. This trail includes the decisions made, the means, place, and procedures of data collection, and hurdles that arose and how they were managed. This transparency allows reviewers to assess these processes, correct inconsistencies, and judge the trustworthiness of the study.

Practices

1. **Keep an audit trail** in your journal – the step-by-step processes you used to derive your findings from the data. Choose key steps.

2. **Write a paragraph as an overview:** What is the strongest evidence of the trustworthiness of your study? Why?

Confirming validity

Validity for quantitative studies requires that the measurement tool actually measures what it is supposed to. Researchers need to explain to reviewers why that tool is valid. *Content validity* might mean that the entire content was covered, not just part. For example, in assessing the effectiveness of an online teacher training course, the instrument needs to look at all the content offered, not just part or one class. *Construct validity* might mean that the test measures the concept it was meant to measure. For example, in assessing the effectiveness of a mindset-based intervention to improve 8th-grade math scores, an instrument that measures *liking math* may not measure math *proficiency*.

Practices

1. **List and Write:** Name two possible instruments for measuring what you wish to measure. Why is one better at measuring than the other?

2. **Reflect:** How did you determine which tool to use? What makes you sure you are measuring what you intend to measure?

3. **Pilot study:** Perform a pilot study with your survey questions. **Note in your journal:** Did the responses answer your research questions? What data seem missing? Rewrite a few of the questions.

Confirming reliability

Your instrument should obtain the results multiple times if your findings are to be considered reliable. This does not mean that the instrument measures what it is supposed to. It only means that you will get the same results if you use it again.

Practice for thinking about reliability

Write: Will you claim that your study could be implemented at a different setting with similar results? How confident are you that your instrument will measure the same kind of data at this different site? Explain.

In sum

Your data lie at the heart of your study. Your efforts to ensure its quality pay off when you go to write your Findings/Results chapter. These efforts further pay off when, retrospectively, you rewrite your Methods chapter to detail what you actually did. By triangulating data sources, removing researcher bias, checking and rechecking your coding, and providing member checks, you improve your qualitative data. Keeping an audit trail further increases credibility. For quantitative studies, choosing the best instrument, and testing it, most affects the quality of the data. For both kinds of study, doing a pilot study of your survey or protocol questions has a similar effect of improving your data. The pilot responses bring to the surface the different ways subjects might interpret a question. Rewriting your questions then reduces ambiguity and ensures more accurate data. These steps, described in your final document, help build confidence that the data you have collected accurately answer your research questions.

Part 7: Ethical considerations, positionality, and study limitations

Overview

A number of concerns are aggregated here, each of which requires considerable thought and response. They join together at a high level of generality, as they surface so differently in different studies. Ethical concerns have to do with the potential for coercion, ambiguity, invasion of privacy, loss of income – in general some potential harm or even discomfort to participants or subjects. Positionality has to do with your role with respect to the study, which might create ambiguity or coercion, or simply shade the data so that it is not objective. Study limitations have to do with any piece of the study that undermines its credibility or validity – too few respondents, too few or too homogenous a selection of sites, too short a time frame. All studies have limitations. No study should be approved with ethical concerns.

Ethical concerns

Coercion is foremost among study concerns. No one should feel pressure to participate or experience even the slightest discomfort or hesitation in doing so. Fortunately, the Internal Review Board will do extensive reviews of such a potential, so a few preliminary practices here will suffice.

Practices helping you address ethical concerns

1. **Write:** What ethical protections – such as informed consent, anonymity, impartial and criteria-based recruitment, full disclosure, and voluntary participation without coercion – do you use in your study? For any concern, how will you mitigate it?

2. **Consider and reflect:** What is your position at work with regard to subjects/participants in the study? How might that position create ethical issues or issues with the data (in that participants might want to please you)?

3. **Write a paragraph:** How will you overcome ethically any participant concern about whether they should join your study?

Study limitations

As noted, every study has limitations. You need to detail them, and then explain what you did to overcome them, where possible. Obvious study limitations arise from a lack of time and resources, access, and respondents' willingness to devote time – but readers understand this. Your main concern is to get ahead of critiques of the less transparent weaknesses, perhaps in your criteria for and recruitment of subjects, or in the protocol questions provided (which might be leading or ambiguous) by identifying these concerns before others do.

Practice to uncover limitations

Write: Detail the main study limitations and how you seek to overcome them. What are some of the less obvious weaknesses – like the lack of geographically diverse sites or ethnically diverse participants? Imagine another researcher seeking to implement/replicate your study. What do they need to be aware of?

Working with your Chair

As noted throughout this chapter, you need to work closely with your Chair on each part of this chapter. In your Preliminary Orals, committee members typically focus on the study design, research questions, data collection methods, and the protocols; they typically ask further questions that relate to any possible barriers or ethical considerations. You have likely been discussing with your Chair various elements of this chapter already, but such discussions need to evolve into written arguments that receive careful feedback.

The advice here is to sketch out all of these elements, in writing, for your Chair to review, and to ask for feedback on concerns you noted. Also, ask for concerns they might have. The more you direct the feedback to the trouble spots, the more useful the feedback will be. As always, if a meeting ensues, ask to record that conversation.

Chapter summary

To build a study, you need to be explicit about your design, materials, and processes. As the architect of your project, you present explicit details to a skeptical client – your committee. If your design and materials are not clearly delineated, the building plan will not be approved, as is. The more you have thought through the specifics, the less likely you will be surprised by a committee's questions about barriers and dislocations along the way. Particularly important are ethical concerns, as your project will not be approved if it engenders any sense of harm or even unwanted obligation. In most cases, your Chair will have ensured that the proposal meets requirements, but surprises at Orals can still be disruptive.

The chapter that follows highlights writing up your findings. It prompts the kind of journal entries helpful for writing key pieces. Other texts, including my *Writing Strategies for the Education Dissertation* (2021), provide more extensive general advice on the nitty-gritty of how your study unfolds. This journal, in contrast, activates starting points and practices for composing this pivotal chapter.

5 | Writing up findings

A big leap follows: You have written an approved proposal, passed your Preliminary Orals, and been approved by the Internal Review Board. You have followed your methods and initiated, perhaps completed, the data collection (with road bumps, of course). How does writing enter now?

The Findings chapter is where you present the fruit of your labor, so it is pivotal. If a quantitative study, you need to code (organize and reduce the data), further analyze the data, and decide on what results to present. If a qualitative study, you may have detailed your processes and collected reams of data and analyzed it extensively. But those data do not just turn itself into findings – you can't simply list quotes or observations under general themes. Similarly, for a quantitative study, you can't simply create tables and let them speak for themselves. Even after all the hard work of data collection – then coding, recoding, selecting key data – the task of writing is still a challenge. *Analyses do not just translate into text.* What follows are student retrospectives, on qualitative and quantitative studies, that make this point clear.

Retrospectives from two qualitative researchers

Below, two former doctoral students share their processes with an audience of future student researchers. The first student describes her initial process of coding and generating initial themes for her qualitative study. Her prewriting process alone is very detailed and complex and included note-taking, writing out keywords, and creating written themes she could check against data:

DOI: 10.4324/9781003519904-5

Immerse yourself entirely in your data. I listened to my recorded interviews a total of three times. I read the transcripts repeatedly, took notes, and highlighted keywords and phrases that provided more profound insight into my participants' feelings about my topic. I then categorized their perceptions and used my research questions and frameworks as a guide to develop preliminary codes. After creating codes, I analyzed them to develop initial themes. I reviewed my transcripts and themes again to tease out my findings. A deep understanding of your data and constant revisiting are essential to the data analysis.

Seeking "profound insights," this alumna allowed the initial codes to emerge (bubble up) from continuous absorption of her data. She then "teased out" findings from initial themes: Nothing readymade from coding simply morphed into a write-up. Rather, writing about her data involved a messy, unpredictable, time-intensive process.

A second former doctoral student describes how writing intersected with coding, helping her to develop her "story":

I started by taking one "code" and finding the quotes, then writing … then editing, then going on to another code. I also outlined my path through findings to map what I was hoping to demonstrate. The more I read and listened to the words, the more they started to fall into categories. I tried to write succinct statements for findings and prove my finding – what is the story I want to tell?

This alumna reflects on how formulating the code *in writing* drew her back to her data, then led to *editing* that code, then on to another code, and finally to *succinct statements* for her findings. The accumulation of codes, written with evidence, led her to map where she was going – the story itself that she was going to tell.

Retrospective from a quantitative researcher

While quantitative studies may allow more certainty in creating codes than qualitative studies, they similarly have challenges. The data derived depend on the precision of the survey questions. If the questions are not written well, the responses may not answer the research questions. Much of this planning, writing, and revision is upfront, requiring piloting and significant rewording. So, writers need to seek support before administering the survey. An alumnus shares the following details and advice about his study:

> Since my study was quantitative, I utilized research methods classes and tapped into my professional contacts to create and pilot a questionnaire. I arranged cognitive interviews with classmates, which helped refine my questions. Collaboration with various stakeholders – dissertation chair, professors, statistics tutors, site location personnel, directors – formed a vital support network. Try to overcome any reluctance to ask questions. Also, expect obstacles and have contingency plans. For software needs, trial and error led me to SPSS, introduced by a professor. Unfortunately, analyzing data without proper cleaning was a setback, emphasizing the importance of constant communication with the chair. In your last year, continue to reserve special days, such as Saturdays, just to write. Connecting with a special classmate/friend fosters mutual encouragement and accountability, guiding both of you toward successful completion.

Even with extensive pre-study preparation, including piloting and rewriting his questions, the alumnus encountered later setbacks. These include *cleaning* the data – removing or correcting overlapping, inaccurate, irrelevant, unclear, or incomplete wording, before analysis. Furthermore, he still had to decide on a story to tell – what data to include and how to discuss it. He recommends reserving special days "just to write."

This chapter features some journaling practices pivotal to writing your findings/results. The entries will not turn your data into full text, but they will give you some essential practice and some usable pieces. The practices at times distinguish qualitative from quantitative work, but most of the practices apply to both designs. For both, writers need to tell the story of their data.

Part 1: Initial brainstorming and writing about your data

Overview

Throughout data collection, you take valuable notes in your journal, your *audit trail*. It may be useful to create a **separate section in your journal** dedicated just to writing about your processes – how you collected the data, what the data indicate, and any barriers to collection you had. These journal entries prove useful in writing up findings, when you explain your processes. Readers want to know about what went on – to assess your findings in context.

You can also use your journal for initial brainstorming about findings – your thoughts about the data collected, their meaning and use. Again, these entries will be useful for later drafting: Ask yourself, what significance did a quote or document first hold for you?

Initial journal writing can include other *on-the-spot thinking* as it surfaces. You might note how you identified representative evidence (i.e., quotes, observations, or documents). You might be drawn to an interesting anomaly in a table. You could also capture thoughts on how data from different sources confirm or disconfirm findings. Even at this early stage, you might find yourself weighing alternative structures for presenting data. This initial brainstorming helps you develop materials and strategies for putting into full text what you have found. Journaling promotes as well as embodies your thinking.

From codes to initial text

To get from code to initial text, a good practice is to take a code and explain how you identified it in your data (or why you selected it if it was pre-set in a quantitative study). The initial practices below will not give you final written products but rather the experience of working up from the data to codes and then to findings.

Practices

1. **Take journal notes:** After surveying your data, Identify a tentative code; then **list** different kinds of data that form the code. If the study is purely quantitative, present the numbers that comprise the code.

2. **Write:** In full text, explain: How do the data (possibly different kinds of data) support the code? Or, if data are quantitative, how was non-numerical information grouped and assigned a numerical code?

3. **Take notes:** Using the above model, identify two more codes (pre-set or derived), with the data that support each, and *compose a possible finding*.

4. **Write a bare-bones paragraph:** Produce a description of your finding, and substantiate that finding with the evidence from your data.

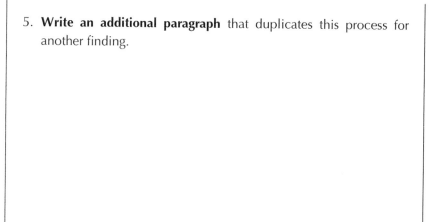

5. **Write an additional paragraph** that duplicates this process for another finding.

Identifying persuasive quotes, observations, or sections of documents

You choose which evidence to share based on how concrete, compelling, and relevant it appears. Not all evidence is strong. For quantitative studies, some of the data may overlap or not respond to the research question. These data do not need to appear in your results. For qualitative studies, select only the most clear and persuasive evidence (without cherry picking to avoid contrary evidence). The more concrete and detailed, the more powerful. And choose only what you need. Do not overwhelm your reader with quantities of quotes or tables, despite their vividness. Rather, identify *representative* evidence.

To indicate how your selection is representative, state how often the idea appeared in your data or that it represents an idea repeated across different kinds of participants. Also, pare down the quote or document itself to its essential elements, using ellipses for deleted words. Avoid cluttering up your reader's mind with the inessential.

Practices for identifying key qualitative data

1. **Take notes:** Write in your journal what you judge to be the strongest evidence for one of your key codes. What words or phrases (or images) most jump out at you? Why? What do they show?

2. **Write:** How is the evidence *representative* of your collected data? Explain.

3. **Write:** Is there any contrary evidence? How will you discuss that evidence in light of your more representative evidence?

4. **Brainstorm with notes:** Does your strongest evidence make you want to rethink your code?

5. **Quick-write a** paragraph in which you use only compelling data to formulate a code.

6. Using the example below, list key quotes under a code.

Example: coding of compelling data

Below are powerful data from interviews with 12 incarcerated adults about their letter writing from jail – a communication distinct from phone calls or visits:

Saying the unsaid:

- *"Not a lot of people share verbally, but paper? That's a whole different thing."*
- *"If I like got these things I want to say to these people and I can't talk to them...I express myself in the letters."*
- *"It's the only way to be heard. It really is."*

These data sharply contrast letters and talk, and the code, *saying the unsaid*, heightens the paradox. The writer then coded other powerful quotes as *deep thinking*:

- *When I'm just talking, I'm just talking...But when I'm on the letter, I'm thinking.*
- *When you write letters, especially from jail to the streets, you're saying what you're feeling, and you have to articulate it. So, it takes a thought process.*

Codes group together representative data into a category.

Practice

For your own study, list the strongest, most representative data and separate it into two codes.

Identifying strong data for a quantitative study

The data derived from a quantitative study depend on the precision of the survey questions – their likelihood of evoking appropriate response – and their fit with the study's research questions. If the survey questions were not clear, the data will not answer the research questions. Much of this writing, review, and revision was upfront, requiring piloting and significant rethinking. Once you have administrated the survey, your first step is to analyze your data with respect to your research questions and look for the strongest results. But first, you need to clean the data.

Practices for identifying and analyzing your quantitative data

1. **Explain:** How did you clean your data, which involves making sure it is correct, complete, labeled appropriately, and not overlapping?

2. **Provide details:** What program did you use for analyzing your data? Why did you choose that program? What weaknesses does this program have?

3. **Take notes:** What results are the most conclusive in answering one or more research questions? Describe those results.

4. **Identify:** Which results were the most significant, given previous research? Why?

---

5. **Identify glitches:** Is there overlapping, unclear, or inaccurate data? If so, what survey questions seem responsible for this problem? How will you describe the glitches?

Assessing possible structures

Before you take a stab at writing up this chapter on findings, you need to assess some possible structures. For qualitative work, will you develop by theme? Describe an evolution? Categorize by different kinds of use? Describe individual cases? Or, typical for quantitative studies, will you answer your research questions, one by one? If you have too many results, themes, cases, or histories, what will you combine or leave out?

Compression is important. If yours is a quantitative study, you need to identify the most significant data and decide on what data you can eliminate: You might need to combine less significant data. You also want to avoid table after table, without a plan for best answering your research questions. If yours is a qualitative study, you need a structure that will help you feature the most surprising or in-depth findings, but not overwhelm your reader with details. You have a number of choices, so avoid settling on the first that comes to mind.

Practices for selecting a structure

1. **Notes:** Identify several possible structures for your finding/results, detailing each. What are the advantages of each structure, in terms of answering your research questions?

2. **Outline:** Create a tentative outline for a promising structure. What data would fit where? Refine the outline.

3. **Reflective Notes:** For each structure, how would you combine or exclude some of the less significant data?

4. **Reread and rethink:** Reread your Problem Statement for your initial objectives. **Write:** How will a selected structure best support your objectives? **Explain why**, as if writing to your Chair.

5. **Reread and revise your outline:** Then send it to your Chair for review.
6. **Record:** What did your Chair say about your proposed structure?

In sum

Initial journaling helps you invent, assess, and plan what will be the most significant part of your study – your findings. You use writing to think, especially to brainstorm and outline. You also use writing to home in on your evidence – assessing it, selecting it, reducing it, tying it to codes – using it to answer your research questions. In the process, you learn to think about your thinking, as you have a record of your thoughts. The next step is to implement the plan and to draft write, in full text, some key pieces of the chapter.

Part 2: Getting started, writing sections, and then drafting your findings/results chapter

Overview

Once you have created a structure, and had it approved by your Chair, it can be difficult to get started with your writing. You are presenting what readers most want to know – which puts some pressure on you as a writer. But rather than rushing through a full draft chapter, start drafting a single piece. This might be an introduction, the context of the study, a summary of your key findings, or even a key section that is vivid in your mind. You just need to get started – get some writing on the page.

Introduction and summary of findings

An introduction is often the easiest place to start. Most findings/results chapters open with a restatement of the study objectives, data sources, processes, and research questions. Such an opening recaptures, looking back, the original impetus of the work. Try to make it reinvigorate the reader. You might also start with the context of the study – its setting, population, or institution. These descriptions do not have to use dull, repetitive terms – you can add vividly observed details that place the reader in that setting.

After the introduction, the chapter likely summarizes the key findings. These might be divided into findings or results that confirm what we already know and those that add to what we know. It can also open with the most challenging/surprising finding that emerged. Furthermore, both qualitative and quantitative studies typically provide a preview (or roadmap) of what you will discuss – and in what order. However, the quantitative study is typically very direct in how the study answers the research questions, following them one by one.

Practices

1. **Write in your journal:** Restate briefly the purpose of your study. **Add:** How did you as researcher go about the study? (Add details to what you have in the Methods chapter.)

2. **Write** a detailed paragraph on the context of the study – the study environment, the problems that surfaced, the type of site and participants. Include study processes – how the work unfolded.

3. **Write a summary** of your key findings, in a way that reflects your chosen structure (most significant findings; confirming vs. disputing previous research; by themes; case-by-case; research question by research question).

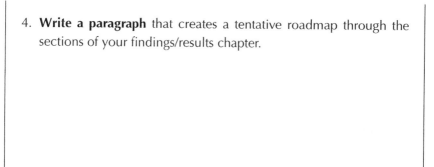

4. **Write a paragraph** that creates a tentative roadmap through the sections of your findings/results chapter.

Refining your structure as you go: innovative adjustments in presenting data

The amount of data you collected may seem overwhelming. Even with an approved structure, and a solid roadmap, you may need to innovate as you present key pieces of this chapter. If you did seven cases of individuals, perhaps you decide to present three as extended cases, representing a continuum, and the rest to discuss together to show themes. Or if you are looking at group behaviors, perhaps several key behaviors surface continuously, so you decide to detail those and subordinate others. In another innovation, you might note that findings concerning barriers seem to present chronologically, so you decide to write them up as "a day in the life of..." – to represent everyday challenges. As a reminder, dissertation writers are often asked to reduce the number of cases, themes, tables, or data – to combine or eliminate the less supported ones.

Beyond *reducing* data, the sheer amount of data may require you to innovate ways to *integrate* data. This is especially true for a mixed-methods study. You might decide to feature a key theme, supported with telling quotes from interviews, and then integrate numbers from your survey questions for further support. For a purely quantitative study, typically presented in tables, you might integrate data from several survey questions into one table. For qualitative studies with different data sources (e.g., observations, focus groups), you may innovate ways to integrate the data from these different sources. You likely need to check such decisions with your Chair.

Practices

1. **Reflect:** What refined structures could present your key findings but not obligate you to present all of your data?

2. **Write** as a journal entry a rationale for how to reduce the data to the essentials.

3. **Take notes:** What options do you have for integrating data to support your findings? What is the advantage of each?

4. **Outline:** As your writing evolves, create a new roadmap through your findings that simplifies your presentation.

5. **Reflect and journal write:** Which roadmap do you think will best present your findings? Why?

Generate your first full draft findings chapter

You may have significant pieces and a doable plan for this chapter, but getting a full chapter draft is still a challenge. Try rereading and writing as you go but not stopping to edit – in order to move forward with drafting your full findings chapter. Writing produces more writing, more thought. As underscored elsewhere, *writing **is** thought, not the aftermath of thought*. Indeed, you think as you write, and then rereading prompts more thought. So let the momentum of producing ideas push you on, without too much stopping to revise. At this stage, you want ideas, as well as the evidence they elicit, to flow freely; you don't want to block that flow with worries about editing.

Practices for drafting

1. **Speed-write** two consecutive paragraphs without stopping.

2. **Reread to write:** Rather than editing that section, reread it quickly, primarily to activate more writing. **Make notes** in your journal on new ideas and where you will go next.

3. **Plan several sections ahead with a new list:** What series of claims will you likely take on next?

4. **Keep remembering the "why" of this study:** You are not mechanically following your research questions and listing evidence. You are evaluating data, based on your initial goals, and then composing a presentation of evidence to support that evaluation. Some students mistakenly think that findings are literally "found." They are not. **Write a reminder to yourself** as to why you decided to do this study in the first place.

5. **Complete a first draft:** Using your roadmap, outline, notes, and written sections, compose a first draft of your findings chapter, in a Word document.

In sum

Drafting the full text of your findings chapter requires belief (in your study, in yourself) and perseverance. You believe that the writing will evolve, and you persevere through the plans, steps, pieces of writing, decisions, and uncertainties. You make shifts and adjustments as you go along. You use writing to think. But once you have an outline and then a draft, you have something major to work with, to improve on. The revision stage lies ahead.

Part 3: Adding, integrating, connecting, and sharpening the evidence of your first draft

Overview

Once you have a full first draft, read it through, looking critically at your evidence. Revisit the supportive data you have selected, assessing whether it shows the finding you say it does. This might mean adding – possibly replacing – quotes, tables, or other supportive documents; it could also entail making your findings less generalized. Furthermore, as advised earlier, try to integrate evidence from more than one source, triangulating (confirming or qualifying) your evidence. For specific places, look to sharpen how you introduce evidence, such as a table or a quote, and then be sure to detail afterward how it supports your claim. In sum, you need to sharpen your argument: Tell the reader what to take from the data.

Revisit your evidence

You want to underscore how your evidence tells a story. What pieces are the most convincing that you have collected? How do you make those data more fully tell a story? Here is an example of an effective *lead-in* and *follow-up* to a strong quote. It comes from the action research study on principals endeavoring to shift a school culture to one of inclusion for students with disabilities. The writer concludes with how representative the quote is.

Although district messaging was influential, [principals] stated that messaging had to start with them. It was essential that staff understood that inclusion originated with the principal, not a faceless district mandate. Allison elaborated: "I've never told my staff that it's the district wanting me to do this. Or parents pushing for this. Otherwise, it would get brushed off. I believe in this, so you should too." Allison shows an awareness of the power of her personal beliefs and her connection to her staff. Leaders who fail to "own" inclusion are

messaging that it is not worth taking seriously. It was equally important that messaging stayed the course. All members spoke to inclusion
as feeling like a marathon, not a sprint.

The writer here offers a *lead-in* to the quote – that messaging (about inclusion) needs to start with the school principal. The quote then substantiates
the writer's claim, animated by the participant's passionate voice. The writer
then analyzes what the quote shows – the power of personal beliefs ("own-
ing" inclusion), indicating the seriousness of the message from the principal.
The end comment, with its image of a marathon of effort, wraps up the story.

Practices for further heightening the evidence

1. **Rewrite:** For a section on a finding, select different, perhaps
   more compelling evidence, and use your journal to rewrite and
   strengthen that section. Add a *lead-in* and a *follow-up* comment,
   directing the reader to see what the evidence shows.

2. **Integrate evidence:** Choose a claim, sharpen its wording, and then
   combine evidence from more than one source to firm up your
   claim. Qualify with any outlier evidence.

3. **Add:** In a *follow-up* to any quote, explain what it shows and how
   representative the evidence is. In a *follow-up* to a table, direct readers' attention to specific data and what the data show.

Revisit how you connect evidence to your research questions

You might be telling a vivid story and using compelling evidence, but that story might not answer your research questions. Review every part of your developing Word draft, in particular the evidence, to ensure that the story you tell relates to those questions. Have your research questions always before you. Write out potential connections in your journal.

Practices

1. **Reflect and identify in your journal** any place in your chapter draft where your evidence might not tie explicitly back to a research question.

2. **Add further notes:** For these key places, clarify how the evidence (or different evidence) does support the finding and does answer a research question.

In sum

Your evidence is where the rubber hits the road. The selected data need to be concrete and compelling, to derive from different sources, and to stand for the dataset as a whole. Look for places where you can add supportive data and make your case more airtight. Then check that the discussion surrounding those data directs readers' attention to what that evidence shows. Remember to tie the evidence clearly to a finding and the finding explicitly to a research question. With a first draft completed, re-examined, and revised, consider sending it to your Chair.

Part 4: Reread to rewrite

Overview

Likely, after submitting to your Chair a complete first draft, you have received comments about potential changes. To rewrite further, you will need time between your submitted draft and your next draft, to absorb any comments. When writers plunge into revision, they typically "read in" what they intend, uncritically. To respond to Chair comments, you need a distanced, critical lens, along with potential comments from other readers. What follows are suggestions for your next complete draft.

Allowing time between drafts

Even without commentary from your Chair, you likely need time between drafts. This way, you will be less inclined to make assumptions about what you meant. After a number of days, on rereading you may find yourself befuddled by some things you wrote. You may also be surprised by how good some places sound. You are assuming the role of the reader.

Practices, once you resume work

1. **Write:** Summarize in your journal your Chair's comments.

2. **Read** your full draft out loud. **Note** in your journal a few places where you struggled to understand what you read or where the writing seems overgeneralized or unsupported. **Note also** where it reads fluently.

3. **Revise:** Take a problematic paragraph from your Word document and revise it for clarity, evidence, connectedness, or other problems that reflect your Chair's input. Let your mind stretch. **Then, in your journal write:** How did you apply your Chair's comments to this one section?

4. **Learning:** What did you learn from revising the paragraph? **Note this learning in your journal**.

Rereading to distinguish analysis from interpretation

Each piece of data, or table you present, requires a close analysis – to help pinpoint for readers what you see. As noted earlier, for each quote or data-set, you first introduce the data (you target what readers are to look for), and then after presenting it, you identify what in the data makes your point (so that readers see what you see). Your addition here is not considered interpretation. Rather, the lead-in and end comment comprise your analysis: You are tying the data to your point. Be sure to review that analysis, to ensure that you are not over-interpreting – hyping what you see by overgeneralizing, editorializing, or jumping to conclusions. Apply that same concern to larger claims about data.

Practices in analysis

1. **Review your lead-ins and end comments**: Identify a quote or piece of data (or table) where your commentary seems questionable. Ask others for their analysis. If you encounter disagreement, **revise** the *lead-in* and *end comment* so that they state more objectively what the evidence shows.

2. **Review the logic of how evidence connects**: In a place where evidence seems not to connect, write to reconsider: What is your claim? What seems problematic with your analysis? Use your journal to revise this section.

Another check: eliminating bias

Bias creeps in through many doors: interviewer bias, reporting bias (the interviewee wants to please the interviewer), confirmation bias (you want data that confirm what you hypothesize or wish to prove), how you discuss what the data show, and who you feature in your cases. Significantly, all research has some biases. You work to eliminate all you can. Your findings need to state explicitly what you did to counter bias.

Practices

1. **Reflect and write:** What strategies helped counter any tendency to pick data that supports a hypothesis or desired outcome?

2. **Write:** What strategies eliminated response bias (interviewees give the "correct" or socially desirable answer)?

3. **Write:** Review in a paragraph how you kept records, reanalyzed data, used another coder (if you did), or checked with colleagues to reduce bias. What do you think was most effective in reducing your bias?

When to submit your next draft to your Chair

When you have outlined, written, and rewritten your first draft, it is key to get the revised work again reviewed. If you have a colleague who can review your work, that would be a helpful start. Most valuable would be to submit the work to your Chair for another full-draft review. Be prepared for a stiff critique. It is part of the process.

Practice

Write: First, do your own hypothetical critique: What might be the key weaknesses of your findings/results draft? What recommendations would you give to yourself for next steps? Remember, this is just practice.

Working with your Chair

Your Chair is really your partner in this process, the only person, other than yourself, who is intimately involved in seeing you produce a high-quality academic study – and in your finishing. So, guard that relationship well. That partnership has many facets, but at this key juncture, it clearly involves setting up a time frame for submissions, respecting a Chair's time, showing appreciation for their input, taking notes on or recording what is said, responding to the advice, and discussing in advance the best times to meet and best methods of communicating. For each meeting it helps to have an agenda and to follow up meetings with a note that includes any questions or reminders. While these concerns have always been in place, they are particularly important in writing up findings.

Practice: keeping notes on your Chair's suggestions

1. **Recordings and notes:** What overall did your Chair suggest? What are you to do next? Why is that the crucial next step?

2. **Write out any questions as they occur:** What questions do you have that you can raise next time?

3. **Notes to yourself:** How will you accomplish the next step in the process?

4. **Write to remind yourself:** How do your findings relate back to your original purpose? What in your Chair's response helps you to better realize that purpose?

Writing and rewriting until it gets done

The "next step" involves a series of potential draft revisions. *Revision as re-vision-ing* is indeed the motto for your findings chapter. This chapter typically gets written and rewritten, under the guidance of your Chair. You may have a treasure trove of data, but unless you can reduce it, analyze it, synthesize it, and use it effectively to argue for your findings, your claims will leave readers cold. Be prepared for a series of drafts. As the evidence strengthens, and the presentation becomes more focused, the study becomes more compelling. One last thing to check: return to your chapter opening and rework it. Add extra purposefulness to that opening.

Revisiting your opening

With a substantial draft, rewritten and (mostly) approved, you know how this chapter unfolds: You also know what matters about what your study found. Stepping back, now write a lead-in that breathes life into your findings. See the model below. It comes from the action research study, noted earlier, on the co-training of k-12 principals on the issue of inclusion. She could not have written this lead-in before completing her Findings chapter. Reflecting on her story, she introduces her study findings in the context of the wider problem of dual systems in formal education. The new lead-in adds precision and power to her presentation.

> The history of formalized education is one of dual systems, special education sitting apart from general education, contributing to significant achievement gaps for students with disabilities. This study is the story of merging systems. It involves engaging school leaders with special education backgrounds as action research members – to educate school leaders without such experience ... in building inclusive schools and thereby reducing the variability of student experiences. The underlying belief of the study is that by studying standard inclusive practices, **all** school leaders might better address the more complex issues surrounding special education. Developing standard practices would be key to reducing the cognitive overload associated with leading special education programs as a whole.

Here, the writer discovers a new way to compress and characterize her story – as one of "merging systems," an image that carries the weight of what follows. Hers is a unique action research study, one that joined together principals who had received special education training to guide a group of principals who had not. Together, the trained principals co-created an education model for developing standard practices for building inclusive schools – for merging systems. This rewritten opening now serves to depict, contextualize, and justify her study, in reflective language that sets up her findings.

Practices

1. **Rewrite** your own introduction to your findings/results chapter. What image or concept could you use that distills the story? How could a quantitative study opening introduce the story of its results?

2. **Create a different introduction**, from a different point of view. Invent a different image or way in to your story.

3. **Evaluate:** Which version do you like best? Why?

Summary of the chapter

Writing your findings/results chapter is a challenge – but it is also its own reward. Your work here comes to a head: You have had to identify, analyze, and write about your data, and then shape those data into key findings.

Multiple skills were involved. Fortunately, once you have a first draft, you can reassess and then envision next steps. Given the complexity of the writing – analysis and reanalysis, multiple drafts, redirections from your Chair – it requires perseverance and belief.

A word to the wise: Some students want this chapter done quickly, and they charge too far ahead, with what they think are definitive findings. In the end, they may have to jettison long pieces, when their writing veers off-base. Try to slow down, put in the reflective time, let the writing flow but then review it, check with your Chair, and learn from the process. Every part of the journey has something to teach you. As an inspiration, consider what a thoughtful former student writes about the process:

> The process of discovering what you need in Chapter 4 [Findings] is a bit like writing a song. As a musician, I'm always hearing melodies or am inspired by sounds or ideas I come across throughout the day. When it comes to putting a song together, I pull from those sources, many which I've either recorded on my phone or lyrics I've put in a notebook, and then start constructing something. I usually don't like the first few versions I come up with, but eventually, something starts to form that I can live with. But the key is that all of it came from outside of me, much like Ch 4. Even though we create the outline and the questions we want to address in our first three chapters, the ideas and "music" come from the people we engage through interviews and surveys. When it comes time to put all of that data together, you need to let the story you're telling in Ch. 4 emerge like a song. It'll be scrappy at first, but you have to get something down to get started. Then you just start building from there and may not be happy with what you've come up with until you've written multiple drafts. Eventually, you'll reach a narrative that was driven by your initial interest but is defined by those you get data from. Let that drive the process and see where it takes you.

This alumnus here champions the openness, learning, slow emergence, and review, in creating a Findings chapter. It is your song, and although the elements come from "outside" you, the music is yours.

6 Writing the Discussion

The Discussion chapter is where your own voice surfaces. The floodgates open, and you begin interpreting the story – adding emphasis, implications, and recommendations. A good motto to remember: *the Findings chapter reports, while the Discussion chapter interprets:* The writer gives meaning to the data.

Given this latitude, the Discussion chapter offers a spectrum of possibilities – choices for different takes on the story. While you also admit limitations, you mostly share what your study means or adds. For instance, you might discuss how your work shifts our thinking or actions, activated by an unexpected finding. You can also make recommendations for practice, especially given a history of failed interventions. Furthermore, you could discuss implications for specific groups affected by your work – and possibly the impact on you personally. Multiple possibilities arise. But how does one start?

Part 1: Openings

Overview

You can open the Discussion chapter in many ways. A typical way is to return to the study's original purpose; you then highlight, from an aerial view, your key findings. For even a standard opener, your voice can be highly personal or more down-to-earth, conversational; it can be more speculative and reflective or more modest and judicious. While you avoid appearing demanding or proselytizing, you typically project self-assurance. You are now the expert.

DOI: 10.4324/9781003519904-6

Some model ways in

You can begin in other ways than to summarize purpose. But let your voice create a sense of meaning. Try out a few opening sentences similar to the ones below.

1. Of all the findings from this project on X..., the most surprising was Y.... (**state upfront**)
2. I went into this study thinking X....I found, more deeply than I expected, Y.... (**personal context, preview**)
3. Most families have an insecurity from which they have yet to fully heal, and the American education [health, legal, political] system is no exception.... (**generality; truism**)
4. The idea for this study came to me.... (**personal origin of study**)
5. Even though the survey indicated that all support services were very helpful, respondents revealed that.... (**introduce survey data right away; state disparity in data**)
6. Katie Meyer is dead. She was found unresponsive in her residence hall on March 1 and was determined to have died by suicide. (**dramatic opening; showing problem of study**)
7. Before this study, it was known that 98% of nursing programs had already integrated simulation technology into their curriculum; however, the percent of simulation use at each school was not known, nor was the impact of simulation use on enrollment. (**what is not known**)
8. Even though Latinas enroll in college at a higher rate than all other female ethnic groups except for Asian women, they are retained and graduated at lower rates than all other female demographics. (**one-sentence summary of problem**)

Practices

1. Choose two alternative sentence openers and **write** a short opening paragraph for each.

2. Which one do you prefer? **Reflect:** Why do you prefer one over the other?

3. Use the above exercise to begin in yet another way.

4. **Write** an opening paragraph that begins with your early motivation for doing this study. Perhaps cite a personal experience.

Summarizing your findings

Somewhere upfront in this chapter, you typically recap your study's purpose and key findings – the ones you will interpret. Some Chairs require this recap as the chapter opener. Avoid repetition from earlier chapters by giving your purpose a wider context – and your findings new import.

Practices

1. **Write:** Restate succinctly the purpose of your research. If this is a qualitative study, give new context to that purpose (its fit with larger studies, perhaps). If quantitative, stay closer to the original language.

2. **Reflect:** What findings/results do you most want to discuss? (You can choose what to discuss and what to ignore.) Why?

3. **Quick Notes:** What findings seem less important, those you may want to ignore or downplay? Why do you see them as less important than you did originally?

4. **Describe to others and then quick-write:** After an oral rehearsal, quick-write a draft of your introduction and summary. State anew your study objectives and key findings or results.

Other summarizing openers, for quantitative studies

Quantitative or mixed-methods studies typically open differently from qualitative studies and have less latitude with voice. Most often, the Discussion chapter opens with a short Introduction – perhaps stating procedures – and then summarizes the results to be discussed, mostly in an objective voice. The opening might also list the sections to come, including limitations and implications. Overall, there is less speculation about meaning and more consideration of how the results advance previous research.

Practices

1. **Quick-write** an introduction, in an objective voice, of your key procedures for a mixed methods or quantitative study.

2. **Summarize** the study's major results, those you will comment on. **Include qualifiers:** What intervening variables will you discuss?

3. **Identify your section titles**, for example, *Contributions to previous research*; *Results* (those that best answer the research questions); *Study limitations*; *Implications for future research*.

Discussing qualitative findings with an early example

To engage readers in *significance*, you might begin explaining your data with a defining example. While the data needed to first appear in your Findings chapter (no new data are introduced here), its reappearance in the Discussion chapter might now seem more striking. You thus spotlight that evidence. The example might then begin your story – previewing the kind of significance you will attach to your findings.

Practices

1. **Identify and detail closely:** Having chosen a vivid example from your data, what is the meaning of the example?

2. **Add:** How does the example connect to the larger significance of your findings?

Beginning with theory

You can also turn to theory. You may have begun this study immersed in, and driven by, a theory. Examples include stereotype threat, engagement, mindfulness, critical race theory, sense of belonging, and adaptive leadership. The possibilities are extensive. One writer began with the theory of enrollment management, for community college leaders facing decreasing enrollment. Still another opened with distributed leadership. Yet another, who looked at universities' increasing reliance on online teacher training, began with diffusion of innovation.

There are multiple possibilities for using theory as a point of departure. The theory likely governed the development of your project, and was discussed in your Literature Review as part of your theoretical framework. Consider explaining early in your Discussion chapter how that theory framed your study and shaped your findings and how it now helps you unveil the significance of your findings.

Practices

1. **Summarize your study** by restating/explaining the key theory governing your study.

2. **Write a paragraph:** Review the role of theory in your study. How did it govern the questions, the procedures, the findings, and now the significance?

3. **Add**: How might theory have limited the study's findings?

Highlighting the study's contribution and previewing the chapter

You can also consider jump-starting your Discussion chapter with the study's *contribution* and then laying out your roadmap for the chapter. This choice may be especially appropriate if you have investigated a major policy change or innovation, one that is changing the lives of many. The example below is from a study that investigated the early effects of AB 705, the California assembly bill that removed remedial courses from all California Community College transfer requirements. The student was concerned with the resulting experiences of underprepared Latina/o/x students who entered credit-bearing, transfer-level math classes and were offered "corequisite" classes as remedial support. What follows is only part of her opening, leading to her summary and recommendations.

This study contributes to the scholarly literature on the experiences of Latina/o/x students in community college math and confirms some initial recommendations about the design of corequisite math classes. In addition, insights from my study provide a complex understanding of the emotional and intellectual experience of students directly entering transfer-level math courses as they deal with feelings of anxiety around math that have the potential to derail their aspirational academic goals for themselves and their families.

In this chapter, I summarize the significant findings and contextualize them within relevant existing research. I then present recommendations for practice related to AB 705 implementation, identify the limitations of my study, and provide suggestions for future research. To conclude, I present an implementation update and include my reflection on what I have learned from conducting this study.

The magnitude of the change wrought by AB 705 warrants the writer's early focus on the study's contribution, as well as her sober tone – given the potential effect of this bill on the students and their families. As the study has a wide and varying potential readership, the roadmap previews the pieces of this chapter.

In sum

You have a lot of choice in how you begin to discuss your findings. What voice will you project? What opening will you choose? If your study is mostly quantitative, your research questions likely dictate your discussion. If qualitative, the most impactful findings or theories may prompt your writing. But for both kinds of studies, you still home in on the data and findings that lie at the heart of the study. The most important findings/results typically get presented and commented on first.

Part 2: What is the story of your research?

Overview

After your opening, you want to create for the reader your study's *story*, with glosses on that story's meaning (both public and personal). One typical way to accomplish this is to describe how the work unfolded – explaining how your findings answered your questions (or in some cases failed to answer them). The unfolding itself tells a new story. Another storyline is how your work derived from similar research, to which yours adds a piece. Here, you might backtrack to certain foundational literature, which spawned several branches of research, leading to yours. You could thus center your contribution – what your study confirmed or disconfirmed from previous work and what it added. A third way might be to recall the most significant and surprising finding and then discuss why it was so surprising, given existing literature. A fourth storyline could involve conveying the potential impact on various users, especially if you set out to help specific groups. There are many ways to tell your story to spotlight the *significance* of your work. Consider different approaches before choosing one. Writing practices for heightening the story follow.

Integrating a personal narrative

If you choose to integrate a personal story, you might deepen the narrative with descriptions that vivify the work. You could state broadly why you chose to do this work – as well as describe specific experiences, events, and effects that motivated you to investigate this problem. As you revisit the study for significance, you might also add personal meaning to how you developed your questions and to key interpretations of quotes, observations, or other data. You could also consider adding a personal reflection at the end of the chapter.

Practices that personalize the story

1. **Write:** What experiences, observations, or literature made you want to study this problem?

2. **Write:** Which of your key study findings most relate to your personal story and motivation?

3. **Brainstorm and take notes:** How might you integrate personal meaning with public meaning, as you write this chapter?

Emphasizing the story by selecting and combining findings

Not all findings are equal. You can select the most solidly supported and impactful findings to discuss. You are not obligated to discuss them all. If your findings took the form of themes, you could choose those themes that are not only most supported but also most meaningful to users. You could also combine several findings under one umbrella theme, as a student did who wrote about "making the invisible visible" – which she concludes, "describes the [action research] team's discoveries, recommendations, and changes in thinking around the subtle, cultural forms of social exclusion based on SES." When you contemplate your work, ask *what stands out for you*. How might you portray an overarching theme that captures several findings and involves your most telling data?

Practices

1. **Reflect:** Choose a key finding or result. What innovative way can you discuss that finding and present its implications or significance, to drive it home to readers? Explain.

2. **Write in your journal:** What finding is likely the most useful to those who will use this work? Explain.

3. **Identify and write:** What ways can you imagine for combining and emphasizing findings? What do these combined findings imply?

4. **Focus on the relation to previous research:** If a quantitative study, how do the results advance or question previous research? What is the significance of that advance?

Telling your story by accentuating impact

As suggested earlier, findings can be discussed individually (avoid choosing too many to discuss) or be united under a few overarching themes. Your commentary might then delineate what those overarching themes could mean for specific sites or groups. The student just referenced had two overarching themes, *making the invisible visible* and *the experience gap* (the distance between the experiences affordable to high Socio-Economic Status (SES) private school students but not to low SES students). She used those two overarching themes for two purposes: to tell the story of her action research team and to explain the significance of her study for independent school administrators and teachers, who were unaware of the subtle discrimination low SES students felt.

Practices for discussing themes by impact

1. **Write in your journal:** After listing 3–4 key themes, which themes could have the most impact? In what ways?

2. **Reflect:** Are there other constituents, not yet considered, who could be affected by your findings/results? Explain who they are and how they might be affected.

3. **Consider and write:** What specific findings might have the most effect on different groups?

4. **Consider further**: What plans do you have for disseminating your findings/results?

Telling the story of the previous literature on this problem

As noted earlier, significance can also be described by how a finding confirms, challenges, or adds to existing literature. The existing studies that prompted your study themselves tell a story. While your Literature Review already details that story, a new, aerial view of the literature can chronicle your work's *contribution*.

Here is an example:

> Most of the existing research on foster youth is focused on areas such as social-emotional development, understanding the child welfare system, and long-term foster youth outcomes. The foster youth at the heart of this [earlier] research tend to be students in high school or adult former foster youth. The intent of [that] research has been to either highlight what high schools can do to support the academic needs of these students to increase high school graduation and college attendance rates, as well as to examine the adverse outcomes that many foster youth experience, or to highlight the personal experiences of foster youth as they have gone through the child welfare system. In looking at the scope of available studies, it was evident that very little research focused on children at the elementary school level or on the teachers who service their needs.

The writer sweeps through existing work and then pinpoints how her research contributes to the larger field of studies on foster youth.

Practices

1. **Reflect:** What finding(s) most contribute to the story of previous work in the field? What was that story? How does your work extend that story?

2. **Write:** How does your work support, extend, or modify *the theory* that has generated much work in the field? Explain.

3. **Anticipate future research:** Given existing research, and your own contribution, where could researchers go next?

Telling the story through recommendations

Making recommendations to solve a problem may also help organize your story. While you may have asked participants for *their* recommendations, and placed these data in Findings, your Discussion chapter would then interpret them: You ask, what do participants' recommendations mean? Using a different approach, this chapter might also offer *your own* recommendations, from surveying all your data. These can then tie back to existing studies, to stress your contribution.

Practices

1. **Take notes:** What possible recommendations follow explicitly from the data you collected?

2. **Write an evaluation:** If you collected participants' recommendations, how do you choose those that stand out?

3. **Write a paragraph:** Describe the actions you recommend, perhaps for specific users. Support each recommendation with specific data from your Findings chapter.

In sum

Discussing findings prompts multiple ways to tell your story – your interpretation of what you found. Try out more than one. Let colleagues read your drafts, to measure the effect of your voice and meaning-making. Review your many entries and jottings above, and see which ones hold your attention. How can you best convey the import of all you did in your study and all that you found?

Part 3: Discussion pieces that are also likely to appear

Overview

A few pieces of writing typically make their appearance in your Discussion chapter (interwoven or written as separate sections). First, readers expect some new detailing of the study's limitations, even missteps:

Known limitations appeared in your Methodology, but other limitations often surface in data collection. Second, committee members may ask for specific social uses: Practitioners' use differs from administrative planning, which differs from policy use; research psychologists use data differently from health administrators. Third, dissertation writers typically speculate about next steps. These are important chapter pieces, which challenge you to reflect and to assess.

Limitations

Every study experiences obstacles that increase its limitations: sample size, limits to geography, low response rates, recruitment problems (especially over-representation of one group among the respondents), unexpected participant reactivity. Missteps appear in the protocol questions, which might have been clearer, and in securing early on the best sites or data sources. A site may even have left the study, perhaps because the time commitment was beyond expectations. The claims you make for your findings, and thus the significance you attach to them, have to be moderated by these limitations.

Readers need to know what you know about blockages – about disappointments you faced, hurdles that appeared, new constraints in time or resources, and unexpected weaknesses in the data collected. Many limitations you knew in advance. Others surfaced as the study unfolded. This explanation and detailing needs to appear somewhere in your Discussion chapter.

Practices

1. **Write:** What is the biggest limitation to your study's findings that you knew in advance? Why?

2. **Write:** What is the biggest limitation to your study's findings that surfaced as the study unfolded?

3. **Reflect and add:** What unexpected events, if any occurred, changed the study's direction? In what ways?

4. **Consider:** What unexpected weakness, if any, appeared in the data? What do you think caused that weakness?

Broad implications and benefits

As noted, you likely add to your Discussion chapter a section on how your findings could affect social practices. This piece could identify and assess how the study might effect change: Policy makers might apply your findings to existing policy; social workers, psychologists, or instructors might apply findings to effect social change in their fields. This detailing of possible benefits can help readers see the spread of significance across different social layers.

Practices

1. **Take notes:** Who are the potential beneficiaries of your work? In what ways?

2. **Speculate and write:** How might each social group act on your findings?

3. **Write a paragraph:** How might each group apply the findings to problems characterizing their field or interest?

Recommendations from study processes

As noted earlier, you may already have a research question, data, and findings on participants' recommendations, which could be recaptured and then discussed. Or you may have your own recommendations to propose and discuss. But in addition, you might construct recommendations that derive from your processes. This piece may fit some studies better than others. But researchers like to make recommendations, and readers like to read recommendations.

Practices

1. **Write:** What key recommendations for practitioners evolve out of your processes?

2. **Ask a colleague and take notes:** Share your findings with a colleague. What recommendations for different processes do they see coming out of your work?

3. **Take notes:** Review key research closest to your own. What examples/recommendations for processes surface from these studies? How might your processes confirm or diverge?

Continued research needs and then next steps

Another typical piece in the Discussion chapter comprises your vision of the continued research need. Your study has uncovered or explained data (or other evidence) surrounding a problem. As a result, you are in a position to see how your work could be disseminated and what researchers could investigate next.

Practices to help envision future action

1. In a short paragraph, **write:** How will you disseminate your work?

2. **Take notes:** What research needs have surfaced from your study? Where are the gaps?

3. **Write:** What kinds of additional studies might help fill these gaps?

4. **Quick-write:** Summarize in a paragraph what you think are the next steps to follow from your own research and who might benefit from such work. Let that speculative piece simmer for some days.

5. **Rewrite:** After reworking other parts of your dissertation, review and rewrite this section on where research should go next and why.

Part 4: Being judicious in your Discussion chapter

Overview

The caution suggested below relates to a key challenge for new researchers: They want to make more of their study findings than the data warrant. The advice here is to stay close to the data, avoid claims the data can't support, give any evidence to the contrary its due, and avoid any pretentions to knowledge, skill sets, unfamiliar professional jargon, and large-scale benefits that you can't support. Also avoid any type of hype you have seen others engage in.

It will undercut rather than push forward your work.

Staying close to the data

What you can legitimately conclude or recommend from your study's findings needs to undergo scrutiny, namely, a comparison with your data. The best advice here is to check out your conclusions with others, in particular your Chair. Be careful not to overgeneralize benefits, especially if there are potential negatives. And if you have quantitative data, be sure that your numbers are statistically significant and that you only claim what the data allow.

Practices for staying close to your data

1. **Review:** Identify one key recommendation or conclusion, and assess whether you are overgeneralizing its import or benefit. Add qualifiers.

2. **Modify:** Being more judicious, modify any overstated recommendation or conclusion to better fit your data.

3. **Identify:** Look for other places in your Discussion where you might be overgeneralizing or claiming more than the data supports. How could you moderate your claims?

Giving contrary evidence its due

Some recommendations require a caveat: Their implementation may be hard, they may come with a big price tag, or they may have negative not just positive effects. For instance, Study Abroad has clear benefits in cultural knowledge and experiential learning. However, the program faces skepticism about the loss of progress in a competitive and rigorous major.

Practices

1. **Identify** two recommendations you think might be unrealistic or have potential downsides.

2. **Write**: Identify the "con" side of one, and explain how best to consider this downside in light of the benefits

3. **Summarize** and acknowledge arguments that could question/moderate your conclusions. Respond with counter arguments supporting your own meanings.

Working with your Chair

As noted throughout this chapter, there is much about the Discussion chapter that your Chair can guide. You face many potential temptations – to claim more than your data support, to ignore contrary evidence, to become strident or imperative (because you care), to claim new knowledge when much has already been studied. Once again, engage your Chair. They will keep you on track. Outline your main points, tie them to key evidence, and present them as a potential first approach to the chapter. Then, with approval, draft the chapter. Once again, expect revisions.

In sum

To review, be judicious in what you claim and how you claim it. Imagine you are writing your Discussion chapter to people who do not immediately agree with you. While you want to make this chapter powerful and engaging, you do not want readers to think that you are being unfair, unreasonable, biased, too quick to make claims, or too prone to overgeneralize and thus distort your evidence. Engage all of your readers, not just those already predisposed to agree.

Concluding the dissertation: lifting the veil

After all of these suggestions and cautions, consider concluding your dissertation with a brief statement of what you felt about your study. Some examples of final paragraphs follow, written by former students who derived intense meaning from their work. In these last statements, they interweave insights that are personal, professional, and research-based.

1. This research was conceived as an extension of my professional experience working in outreach at UCLA for nearly 15 years, as well as because of my role as a father of three Black sons. Originally, I thought that I would conduct research to better understand Black student under-achievement. I am glad that the project became a study of successful students. Far too often researchers and practitioners focus on what is going wrong in the Black community rather than trying to understand and learn from what is working.

2. Now that the study is complete, it is clear that [nursing] schools do have the ability and resources to increase the amount of simulation use. We also see that even with the higher percentage of simulation use to replace clinical hours, there is no significant difference in students' success from before the increase to after the increase in use ... The issue of the nursing shortage must not only be addressed but resolved within the next few years if the nation is to have an adequate number of healthcare workers by the year 2030. By addressing the shortage of clinical placements, this study aims to help nursing programs and stakeholders with their decision making for future simulation use directives.

3. I would not have predicted that this project would end as it has – with the most interesting part of it being the interaction between three methodologies. Mapmaking, photography, and Participant Action Research – interwoven, together, form the spine of this project. Remove any one of these strands and I do not believe the project stands. The linkages between these methods remain to be further explored and codified, but there are definitely linkages. Much to my surprise, this project was much more a mapmaking project than a photography project.

4. This study enabled me to engage with three areas about which I am passionate: special education, educational leadership, and policy. Early in my career, I became aware of the distinct struggles of students with Emotional Disturbance, and this study offered insight into how policy,

educational leadership, and special education intersect. It highlights the need for a shared construct of knowledge building across all levels of educational authority: from the individual decision-maker up to the policy makers (and back down again). They share responsibility for continually building knowledge and making connections to ensure that students get what they need.

5. This study was very personal to me. It came from my experience, my stress, my hurt. As eager as I may have been to connect with others about similar experiences, it was difficult to hear about others' encounters with racial microaggressions and ways that racial battle fatigue manifested for them. During several interviews, I held back tears. It was saddening and infuriating to hear about many of the participants' experiences, both during Diversity, Equity, and Inclusion (DEI) Professional Development, as well as their overall experiences as their day-to-day experiences as Black/African American educators.

Practice

Write a similar concluding paragraph to your work, even if you have not yet completed the work.

Summary of the chapter

You may feel relief flood you when you reach your dissertation's Discussion chapter. And, indeed, the hard work of data collection, analysis, and findings is behind you. You have a story to tell. Your own voice here takes front and center. While this sounds like easy going, choosing significance, in a credible way, is a challenge: It is not self-evident how you persuade readers of the import of your work.

Some doctoral students take the fallback position of discussing each finding one by one, giving each one equal weight. This approach is probably not the best way to engage and persuade readers, as some research findings are not that prominent. Other students, motivated by a particular goal – use select findings to influence a site, profession, leadership, or practice. These writers have to be careful not to leap too quickly to claims and benefits.

This chapter captures some of the choices you have, especially in voice, openings, telling a story, integrating elements, and building reader trust in your interpretations and implications. The chapter gives you practices to try strategies out and encourages you to use your journal to engage in writing as thinking. The writing practices thus strengthen your content and presentation. The chapter also underscores the key role of your Chair in guiding you, especially as you link your work back to previous research and identify your key contribution. Finally, the chapter provides ways to end: How you end matters.

The next chapter looks at the last step – reappraising what you have. It helps you review, sharpen, tighten, signpost, connect, and edit your dissertation so that readers can move through the various parts with ease. This final chapter gives you practice in all of these skills.

Reader-based writing
Reviewing, revising, sharpening, and editing

The final stage of dissertation writing is often seen as the cleanup stage – the housekeeping, word-smithing, compressing, formatting, mechanical stage. Books abound on rapid, slash-through revising. But rather than seeing this stage as mechanics, try to see it more generously – as the **reader-based stage** – where you revisit your work with the reader's response in mind.

The following practices focus on reader experience – where you can connect, clarify, and signpost what you have written. It provides sentence- and paragraph-level practices to better present your ideas, connect evidence to claim, and point readers in the right direction. *Think of yourself as your reader's trail guide – painting rocks as markers along a footpath.* An opening map never hurts either.

Part 1: Thinking about your reader: giving shape to their overall experience

Overview

Granted, you have been thinking about your reader throughout the entire writing of your dissertation. This is especially true because your Chair – your first and key reader – has communicated with you often about the content of your work. But you now have a complete draft. It is time to ask: What is the *experience* like for other readers who are reading your work from start to finish?

DOI: 10.4324/9781003519904-7

When you consider reader experience, you revise to communicate – simply and directly – with the least amount of distraction, overlap, circumlocutions, or jargon. You also anticipate readers' overall need to hold ideas in mind: So, you smooth out bigger connections, use informative headers, introduce main points upfront, connect evidence explicitly to claims, and keep language consistent throughout. Readers need to have a structure, and a sense of ease going forward, not be overworked or left in doubt. With this need in mind, you revise to make it as *reader-based* as possible for them. While such revisions may sound like housekeeping, they are cognitively challenging – you are rereading your work as would your reader and are now paying attention to their experience.

Helping readers by signposting your big sections – with headings and subheadings

Start with the big picture. Your reader appreciates, first and foremost, previews on where they are going. Your Table of Contents will be their first indicator – but you write that last, just before you submit. Another marker is your headings and subheadings: These preview and guide. Most helpful is to write these headings as claims, not one or two-word topic headings (like *the achievement gap,* or *care,* or *exclusionary practices*), which do not suggest a point and cannot predict well what follows.

Here is an example of transforming a **topic** into a **heading**:

Topic: *Low SES Exclusion*

Heading: *Students make visible the invisible: how low SES private school students get excluded*

Practices

1. **Add or revise** key headings and subheadings in your completed draft. **Reflect on your learning here:** What further guidance does this provide?

---

2. Create an **outline** of these headings. Ask a colleague: Do they form an argument, based on claims, that the reader can follow? **Write:** What did you learn?

3. For several long sections, **create subheadings. Write about what you learned:** How do new subheadings guide the reader?

Shaping readers' experience by sharpening transition sentences

Next, move to paragraph previews – not just headings and subheadings but also opening transition sentences preview arguments for readers. Review once again these key transitions, thinking of these sentences as bridges: They carry the reader over the gulf of relatedness, between sections and paragraphs. Avoid letting the headings do the transitioning for you.

Practices

1. Check out your sentences that open new sections. In your Word document, **rewrite** them to better preview the main point of what follows. **Write in your journal:** What did you learn?

2. Find a paragraph in which your main point seems buried in the middle somewhere. **Rewrite** it as the lead sentence into the paragraph. **Write in your journal:** How does that change affect the reader?

3. **Write as a list** your key transition sentences between sections. Do they indicate a connected argument?

4. **Rewrite** key sentences here to sharpen connectedness.

Adding shape: using connecting phrases between sentences

How do individual sentences relate? What clues do readers need to move from sentence to sentence? Readers need guides, throughout, to help them absorb new information as it relates to the old. An obvious way to connect is to list – *first, second, third*. You also have at hand the all-purpose *and, also,* and *but* – as well as the similar *furthermore, in addition,* and *what's more.* Other more nuanced connectors, often used to redirect, include *however, moreover, therefore, thus,* and *consequently.* Many of these indicate logical connections, including a contrary position or an effect.

The choice can often be subtle. When a writer uses *nevertheless* and *on the other hand*, they can lead to a position not necessarily contrary but simply open to other views. But when the writer strongly advocates a position but must present contrary evidence, they use the more oppositional *granted* or *admittedly.* Still other connectors suggest a strong evidential relationship, as with "for example," "this data suggests ..." or "historically, this idea took the form of..." As the writer, you have choices here, but your goal is to help readers better anticipate what follows.

Practices

1. Choose a paragraph and **revise or add** connectors linking each sentence to the sentence before it. Explain why you changed the connections.

---

2. Identify a paragraph where the sentences seem abrupt. Read the paragraph aloud, noting where you hesitated. **Speculate in your journal:** What in the text makes a reader hesitate?

3. **Consider in your journal:** Do you see a pattern in the way you connect sentences? How can you create more informative or guiding connections?

Connecting sentences by linking content

Standard connectors are likely not enough to show links in thought. You may need to use content connectors. The example below shows how linked content words connect sentences.

Systemic and institutional racism *has undermined the* **achievement rates** *of marginalized students. Due to* institutional racism, *Black students continue to lag in* **academic outcomes**, *face harsher discipline, and been assigned to special education at higher rates than their white counterparts. Distance learning may have exacerbated these long-standing* **opportunity and achievement gaps.**

Note how the second sentence connects by using the subject of the first sentence (*racism*) to push forward and how each sentence ends with the key content words, *academic outcomes* or *achievement*. Even the verbs link in a connected, logical chain: *undermined, lag, exacerbated*.

Practices

1. **Rewrite** a series of sentences to link them together by content.

2. **Reread** a key section in your Discussion chapter. **Underline** the content links. **Rewrite** the paragraph here to keep consistent linkages.

Solidifying points by creating summaries as reinforcement

At key junctures, readers also need you to highlight where you have taken them. Otherwise, their experience reading a section may veer from your intent. A concluding summary brings them back to your purpose, affirming and reinforcing your key points.

Practices

1. In your journal, **write (or add to)** a section summary. Match the summary to the content of that section to ensure that it consolidates your key points. **Add a connector** that anticipates what comes next.

2. Quickly review all your section summaries. Use your journal to **list** which ones could still use some work. (Come back to these later and flesh them out for your reader.)

In sum

Shaping readers' experience begins with shaping their expectations. Shaping readers' big expectations comes with your Table of Contents (which you write last), your headings and sub-headings as claims, your key transition sentences, and your end summaries – these anticipate and then confirm your points. Headings are particularly important, as they help readers see where they have been and where they are going next. A collection of them could produce a map. Along the way, you guide readers with other smaller markers, to signpost shifts in direction. These guides are helpful reader-based concerns.

Part 2: Featuring logic: connecting evidence to claims and sharpening contrasts

Overview

A key form of connecting – tightening the logical thread of evidence – clearly improves readers' experience. Often, dissertation writers leave gaps between their evidence and their statement about the evidence. The logical connections seem self-evident. But writers are forgetting the glue holding the evidence to the claim – *why the evidence supports the claim*. These connectors are often called *warrants*. They are the reasons behind your citing this evidence when you make your claim.

Connecting evidence to claims

Logical connectedness increases when you pinpoint, upfront, what the reader should look out for in your evidence, then feature the evidence, and then link specifics to your claim. This targeting eliminates the ambiguity of what in the evidence supports your upfront point. It directs readers' understanding.

Here is an example of a writer making a claim, citing evidence, and then tying evidence to the claim (the warrant), thus tightening the argument. The example is from a study of Black Diversity, Equity, and Inclusion (DEI) leaders' experience of racial battle fatigue during DEI trainings.

A great deal of Jamal's anxiety is rooted in how personal the conversations are in anti-racist DEI PD. It is not in Jamal's nature to share private aspects of his life, especially with those he does not know very well. Yet, as a Black person, Jamal felt as if he were constantly being asked to give personal examples for others' benefit:

> For the sake of the company, we're unearthing trauma ... I felt like the overall goal was to educate white people, and to do that, you need experiences from people of color to educate them. So, **I'm curriculum.** We are curriculum.

Jamal's comments indicate that he felt devalued as a DEI PD (Professional Development) participant, with his worth more tied to being a resource that would facilitate his white colleagues' understanding of race dynamics. Jamal's past traumatic experiences with discrimination and microaggressions had merit, but his personhood did not.

In this example, the writer offers an extensive warrant to tie evidence to claim, thus shaping the reader's experience. He opens with the claim that this Black teacher's anxiety stems from pressure to reveal **prior personal trauma** in DEI trainings. He then cites the teacher's exact words depicting the painful depersonalization in DEI (e.g. *I am the curriculum. We are the curriculum*). Then follows the writer's **key warrant** that explicitly links the quote to the claim about this pressure causing anxiety: The teacher felt devalued – that *being the curriculum* means being seen as a *resource* (for others' benefit), not a *person*. This warrant ties back to the claim that revealing personal trauma in front of others was not this teacher's nature.

You can apply this rubric about claim, evidence, and warrant to your own presentation of evidence.

Practices using warrants

1. Select an important paragraph in your study's findings, where you present key evidence. **Revise by clarifying** the claim, evidence, and warrant.

2. Identify an additional paragraph where your warrants are incomplete. **Write** full warrants for why your evidence supports your claim.

3. **Reflect:** Where warrants are incomplete, what assumptions are you making about your reader's thinking? **Write:** What did you learn from this reflection?

Sharpening contrasts

In writing warrants, you tie claim to evidence and make distinctions, and those distinctions become clearer through sharp contrasts. At times, writers create contrasts that are not mutually exclusive, and the distinctions then blur.

In the above warrant, note the writer's key contrast between the teacher being a **resource** and his **personhood**. How are these concepts distinct? Consider how that contrast helps explain the quote.

Practices in sharpening contrasts

1. Identify places where you make a key distinction. **State:** How are the two mutually exclusive (or not)?

2. **Identify:** Where else in your argument could you make strong contrasts? **Revise** several key places to heighten the distinction.

3. If you spot a blurry distinction, **reflect:** Where is the overlap? Why is the distinction not clear?

4. For the quote below, from the same study, **write:** What is the extended contrast being developed?

For [non-Black] people who are doing DEI work – if they're delusional about the role that they play or their own privileges – they're not stressed out about this [giving DEI trainings] because it's like, "Oh, this is the one time this week I have to think about this." But for me, I'm thinking about it every day.

5. For the above data, **write:** What warrant (reasoning) would you give for how the quote supports the claim that leading DEI trainings causes anxiety for Blacks?

In sum

Much of the persuasiveness of your writing emerges from how tightly you connect your evidence to your claims – your analysis of your data. That analysis is rooted in your logic – identifying claims you can make, citing the evidence, and then tying the evidence to the claim (the warrant). Recall the powerful reader experience that the DEI researcher created through his analysis. These analytic pieces help convince your reader that your data say what you say it does. And a key tool in providing warrants is through sharp, mutually exclusive contrasts.

Part 3: Revising sentences for smooth reading

Overview

To reflect back on two key processes already discussed: (1) You shape your reader's *overall* experience through headings and sub-headings, lead-ins, and summaries – big-picture predictions and connections; and (2) you shape their immediate experience by fleshing out and sharpening your use of evidence through warrants and sharp contrasts. A key focus now is to reread your sentences, as they unfold, for flow and economy.

Flow

Flow (or *coherence*) is the smoothness with which you move readers through your writing. Granted, you have been working on flow all along: Your logical movement between claim, evidence, and warrant creates logical flow. The headings and subheadings create a flow of expectations. You already worked on generic sentence connectors like *however, nevertheless,* or *to the contrary.* Less evident, however, is the key role that *sentence syntax and sentence topics* play in your reader's experience of flow. Syntax choices include varying the placement of parts of the sentence to help readers see what you are emphasizing. By repositioning sentence elements – subordinating some to others – you guide your reader toward significance.

Below is an example of syntax helping flow, in a single sentence. The sentence parts move readers from the less important background information (reduced to an upfront qualifier) toward the most important information – the significance – at the sentence end (in the main clause):

> When international students expand their social network, they increase their self-esteem, sense of satisfaction, and mental health, leading to higher rates of persistence and retention.

Here, the writer opens with the condition (background) and then states the key action (*they increase…*), which leads to the effect (*higher rates…*), placed at the end for emphasis.

Practices

1. Use your journal to **rewrite** one of your longer sentences by placing the less important, background information into the sentence

---

176

opener position and then ending the sentence with the most important information. What difference does that change make?

2. **Identify and rewrite:** Rewrite a paragraph by repositioning sentence elements to increase emphasis and flow.

Flow is also increased by revising sentences to create *consistent topics*. The wording of each sentence needs to keep readers focused on the topic. Below, a previously discussed paragraph (shortened here) illustrates how careful the writer is to keep each sentence on topic:

> **This study** is the story of **merging systems. It** involves engaging school leaders with special education backgrounds as action research members – to educate school leaders without such experience ... in building **inclusive schools**... The underlying belief **of the study** is that by **studying** standard **inclusive practices**, all school leaders might better address the more complex issues surrounding special education.

Note how each sentence keeps the topic of *study* before us: *this study; it; underlying belief of the study; by studying*. Each sentence also keeps the topic of *inclusion* before us: *merging systems; inclusive schools; inclusive practices*. The writer's sentence-level care increases coherence.

Practices

1. Place in your journal a paragraph that seems jumbled. For each sentence, **underline the key topic words. Then note:** Where could you be taking your reader too far afield?

2. **Rewrite** your chosen paragraph, making it flow better with consistent word choices for your topics.

3. Read the paragraph aloud. Does it flow better? (If it still does not flow, speak it, then **change word choices** once more.) **Write:** What did you learn?

In addition to flow, readers also move forward through sentence economy – where you change passive to active verbs, remove unnecessary prepositional phrases, and reduce overlap, jargon, and other distractors. The next section takes these up under clutter.

Economy: removing clutter

Clutter tires readers out. It also fogs the writer's brain so that rereading your own words becomes a strain – *what was it I was getting at here?* While clutter comes in many forms, it generally diffuses meaning, leaving readers (and writers) unsettled or confused.

Here is clutter hiding in the easy-to-recognize form of jargon:

> Associations between attachment security, assessed as a secure base script (SBS), and teachers' social competence ratings were examined in two examples…

What is so tiring and unsettling about this sentence? It is hard to get through. It bunches together prepositional phrases (*between, as, in*) and gives the reader no clue as to their relative import. Active verbs are missing. Actions like *associate* and *attach* hide in nouns or adjectives (*associations, attachment*), and we don't know who is performing them. The main verb is a passive (*were examined*), so the doer is left out of the picture too.

Also problematic, the sentence fills up with **jargon** (*secure base script; social competence ratings*). Mostly, the wording gets in the way of understanding. This is not reader-friendly writing.

Here is another egregious example:

> By understanding and developing sensitivity to the different dimensions of acculturative stress and the impact of social relations on the management of such stress, college administrators can better support the international population.

The reader is tired out by the time they get to the main subject (*administrators*) and main verb (*support*). The reader needs to hack through the underbrush of 26 jargon-laden, introductory words before getting to the writer's point. The revision clears a way through the thicket:

By managing international students' social and cultural stress, college administrators can better support this population.

Only 10 words now precede the main point. Further, the sentence of 32 words shrank to 15, with much of the obstruction removed.

Practices

1. Identify several cluttered sentences, **underlining** the words or phrases that make them feel cluttered.

2. **Note:** What kinds of the clutter typify your writing? **Reflect:** How can you reduce these kinds of clutter?

Diagnosing clutter

Help with clutter can begin with some simple diagnoses: Where is the **action** in the sentence? **Who** or what performs the action (hopefully not an abstraction)? Who or what receives the action? What **prepositional phrases** can be deleted?

Here is a simple example of diagnosing and then revising:

Original: The potential contribution to school engagement of research on student experience has not been fulfilled.

Ask: What is the key **action?** (*contributes* – buried in the noun *contribution*)

Who/what performs the action? (*student experience* – buried in a prepositional phrase)

What receives the action? (*research*, also buried as the object of a preposition)

Number of prepositions gumming up the works? (three)

Revision: *Student experience could contribute to research on school engagement.*

The revision supercharges *contribute*. (The passive "has not been fulfilled" adds nothing.) Fifteen words reduced to nine; three prepositions reduced to two. Clutter gone.

Practices (with removing clutter)

1. Take a problem sentence and underline the key action (it could be hiding in a noun or adjective). Identify the doer(s) of that action (they may be implied). Put the doer and action together as a sentence, and then add only essential modifications. **Rewrite** the sentence.

2. **Quick-write:** How did that process help clarify your meaning?

3. Take a cluttered paragraph and streamline all the sentences. Work to eliminate 30% of the words.

4. Analyze your most wordy sentences: **Write:** What habits create that wordiness?

Reducing clutter helps readers by reducing fog. But it also helps writers say more with less. This advice now turns to why some words matter more than others – in particular, the single, consolidating, high-octane verb.

How key verbs consolidate – but more importantly inform

Verbs typically communicate more than nouns. They embody an action, not a state of being, and require a concrete doer of that action, as well as a recipient of the action; they thus generate more information. As a result, readers better understand the situation (who the players are and who the recipients are). When you rewrite a series of noun phrases into a **single active verb**, you actually add meaning even as you eliminate clutter. Here is an example:

> Since charter school decision-makers have more flexibility in how they build their programs, **variety is found** in hiring practices and in the development of supports and services to meet the socio-emotional needs of students when compared to LAUSD.

This is a **noun-style** sentence, with nouns proliferating – spreading like weeds and taking over the role of adjectives and verbs. The main verb, *is found*, carries the whole sentence. Unfortunately, the passive *is found* diffuses and obfuscates the main actions the writer wants to foreground – namely *build, hire, develop, meet* – verbs hidden as adjectives, nouns, or in modifying phrases. The revision below identifies *build* as the main verb; it then places the doer, namely charter schools, in front of *build*; next, it puts *programs* after *build* as the receiver of the action – what Charter schools build. The rest of the sentence details this core idea, but in terms of specific actions (verbs). This revision toward a **verb-style** makes the sentence more informative and less cluttered:

> Unlike LAUSD, charter schools can build their own programs, so they can hire more flexibly, and develop supports and services, to meet students' socio-emotional needs.

The verbs pop out – *build, hire, develop, meet*. They tell us a lot about what charter schools can do. And the upfront contrastive structure – *unlike LAUSD* – frames those unique actions. Along the way, the sentence was cut from 38 words to 25 words. Less is more.

Practices to foreground verbs

1. Locate a sentence with weak verbs (*to be* verbs such as *is, are, were*; and all-purpose generic verbs such as *have, did*). Then look for strong, informative verbs that may be hiding in nouns. **Revise** the sentence.

2. Take a short paragraph and **revise** all of the verbs. Make them into more informative, active verbs. Eliminate all of the clutter surrounding them. **Write:** What did you learn?

3. Read a before and after paragraph to a colleague. Ask them: Where did your revisions have an impact?

Summary of the chapter

This chapter helps you shape your readers' experience of your work, to make your writing impactful. The practices here help you look through a different lens – *not how to get the writing out but rather how to make it take hold* – by enhancing signposts, previews, transitions, logic, flow, and economy. Attention to this shaping will serve you well over the rest of your writing career.

Summary and final words on this journal for learning

This book, *Dissertation Practice: A Journal for Learning*, ends with a few final thoughts stemming from reader-based writing, namely, the importance of persuasion. Persuasion is the ultimate goal of all writing – to have an effect on those who will read your work, who will use it, and who will take meaning from it. Persuasion requires effort, it is not a set skill. To persuade readers, you need to delve deeply into your topic, to think and rethink what you are communicating. This takes drafting, distancing, reviewing, and more drafting. Final editing then becomes the last step in communicating to others – to help them see what you see.

In contrast, the self-help books that promise a quick, linear dissertation production, that ignore practice and revision, short-circuit the process – tamping down the electricity between word and thought. Writing advice, in general, needs to cut loose from reductionistic formulas that look for shortcuts. Instead, the advice should promote reflection, thoughtfulness, reseeing, and rewriting – encouraging the *Aha* moments of new insight.

As this book has maintained, writing as thinking involves complex processes of communication. You need to *practice* writing (*praxis* meaning the exercise of an art, science, or skill). And you need to keep at it, in nonthreatening environments, such as journal writing. This book can serve as a private journal, guiding some of these practices, giving you the prompts and personal space to use writing to think. As with a diary, the entries belong to you, and you can reread them quietly to yourself, both to remember your thoughts and to move ahead with them. You can keep your mind clear of any worry about assessment. Through this *practice* will come more fluent writing, until the very act of writing naturally generates more thought. The reward of such practice is that both you and your readers will have participated in learning.

Your final words

Take the mindset assessment in Chapter 1 again. Do you still hold the same mindset? What has changed?

References

Dewey, J. (1910/1971). *How we think*. D. C. Heath. Doi: 10.1037/10903-000.

Durkin, D. B. (2021). *Writing strategies for the education dissertation*. Routledge.

Dweck, C. S. (2006). *Mindset: The new psychology of success*. Random House Publishing Group.

Fiore, N. A. (2006). *The now habit: A strategic program for overcoming procrastination and enjoying guilt-free play*. Penguin Group, p. 5. ISBN 978-1-58542-552-5.

Schraw, G., Wadkins, T. & Olafson, L. (2007). Doing the things we do: A grounded theory of academic procrastination. *Journal of Educational Psychology*. 99: 12–25. Doi: 10.1037/0022-0663.99.1.12.

For Product Safety Concerns and Information please contact our EU
representative GPSR@taylorandfrancis.com Taylor & Francis Verlag GmbH,
Kaufingerstraße 24, 80331 München, Germany

Printed and bound by CPI Group (UK) Ltd, Croydon, CR0 4YY
08/06/2025
01897005-0012